The
Wedding Craft
Book

The Wedding Craft Book

Jenni Kirkham

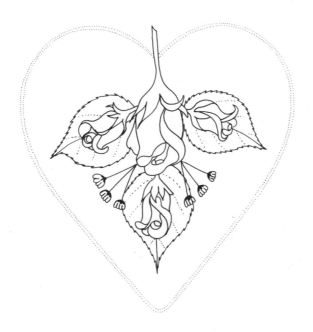

ROBERT HALE • LONDON

To
Gail and Brian

May you always be happy

Acknowledgments
My thanks go to the following people for their help with this book:
- Vivienne Garforth, who made the dresses for the bride and bridesmaid
- Ellen Ender, our hairdresser, who designed the bridesmaid's hair comb
- My models, Gail and Sarah
- Beryl Gordon, who made the wedding cake
- Edward Burbidge, whose video captions inspired the design of the slipcase.
- Philip Burns of Lingtrim Enterprises Pty Ltd, who supplied the Craftlon Ribbon for the slipcase
- My husband Gordon, who took the photographs

Measurement Conversion Chart (1″ = 2.54 cm)

2 mm — 1/16″	7.5 cm — 3″	23 cm — 9⅛″	53 cm — 21¼″	
3 mm — 3/32″	8 cm — 3³⁄₁₆″	23.5 cm — 9¼″	60 cm — 24″	
4 mm — 1/8″	9 cm — 3½″	24 cm — 9½″	65 cm — 26″	
5 mm — 3/16″	10 cm — 4″	24.5 cm — 9⅝″	70 cm — 28″	
13 mm — ½″	11 cm — 4⅜″	25 cm — 9⅞″	75 cm — 29½″	
15 mm — 5/8″	12 cm — 4¾″	26 cm — 10¼″	78 cm — 31″	
25 mm — 1″	13 cm — 5⅛″	27 cm — 10⅝″	80 cm — 32″	
30 mm — 1⅜″	14 cm — 5½″	28 cm — 11¹⁄₁₆″	82 cm — 32¼″	
	15 cm — 5⅞″	29 cm — 11¼″	85 cm — 33½″	
1.5 cm — 5/8″	16 cm — 6¼″	30 cm — 12″	100 cm (1 m) — 39″	
2 cm — 3/4″	17 cm — 6¾″	33 cm — 13″	115 cm — 45″	
2.5 cm — 1″	17.5 cm — 6⅞″	35 cm — 13¾″	120 cm — 47¼″	
3 cm — 1¼″	18 cm — 7⅛″	38 cm — 15″	140 cm — 55⅛″	
4 cm — 1½″	19 cm — 7½″	40 cm — 16″	185 cm — 72⅞″	
5 cm — 2″	19.5 cm — 7⅝″	42 cm — 16¾″	200 cm (2 m) — 78¾″	
6 cm — 2⅜″	20 cm — 7⅞″	44.5 cm — 17½″	260 cm — 102¼″	
6.5 cm — 2⅝″	21 cm — 8¼″	46 cm — 18⅛″	275 cm — 108¼″	
7 cm — 2¾″	22 cm — 8¾″	50 cm — 20″	450 cm (4.5 m) — 177″	

First published in Great Britain 1995

ISBN 0-7090-5637-0

Robert Hale Limited
Clerkenwell House
Clerkenwell Green
London EC1R 0HT

Printed and bound in Hong Kong through Colorcraft Ltd

Contents

Smocked fan (page 13)

Introduction:
The Wedding

In Anglo-Saxon the word *wed* signified a pledge. This became associated with one of the most common contracts made at that time, that of marriage. Initially a civil contract, the presence of a priest as witness led to the eventual incorporation of the marriage service into the rites of the Church of England. For several hundred years this was the only legal way to marry in England, even if the bride and groom were of another faith. Indeed, it was not until 1754 that Jews and Quakers were granted the right to marry outside the Anglican church. Only when the keeping of centralised records of births, marriages and deaths began in 1837 were marriages allowed in places of worship irrespective of religious or sectarian differences. The civil marriage ceremony was also revived at this time. It is against this background of English law and tradition that most of the modern forms of marriage within the English-speaking world have evolved.

Marriage contracts have been made in all societies since history began. Many of the traditions and customs which we observe today originated in ancient civilisations and in other parts of the world. The wedding is full of the symbolism of pagan fertility rites, the belief in evil spirits, and the transfer of property, including the bride herself, from the bride's family to that of the groom. It has also provided an excuse to hold the party of a lifetime for all concerned; an occasion to meet old friends and make new ones, to reminisce with long-lost relations, and to celebrate the end of childhood for the happy couple and a job well done by the parents who raised them.

Every bride seeks perfection on her wedding day; every detail must be just right, and often no expense is spared to achieve this. There are many little touches which can be made by an enthusiastic craftsperson for a fraction of the cost of accessories from a bridal boutique, and within the pages of this book you will find a selection of projects featuring a wide variety of techniques. More ambitious craftspeople may like to read the books listed on page 87, which provide detailed information about such crafts as millinery and floristry, which demand a higher level of skill and knowledge than this book can cover. Also included is a range of books which will augment the techniques explained in the final chapter.

1
The Bride

Ancient custom tells us that on her wedding day every bride should be equipped with:

Something old   to represent the old life
Something new   signifying the start of the new one
Something borrowed   reflecting the aspects of neighbourhood
                         and community spirit
Something blue   symbolising constancy and purity since it
                         is the colour traditionally associated with
                         the Virgin Mary
And a silver sixpence in her shoe to ensure fertility and wealth.

The Wedding Dress
Until recent times the notion of a bride dressed in a white gown which she would probably never wear again was unheard of. A Victorian bride chose her gown to serve as her Sunday best outfit for some years to come, and wore it often after her special day. Practical fabrics and colours were therefore favoured. Today the white dress has become a symbol of purity and, being designed with only one occasion in mind, now displays the finest dressmaking and embroidery skills, skills which might otherwise be neglected in this age when most of us wear casual clothes for all but the most formal occasions.

Often a bride will keep her dress as a family heirloom. The dress should be carefully cleaned, then wrapped in acid-free tissue paper and stored in an acid-free cardboard box in a cool dry place. Another charming idea is to have the dress recut to make a christening gown.

The Veil
Brides in ancient Rome traditionally wore a veil of yellow fabric, a colour sacred to the god of marriage. The custom lapsed after the end of the Roman Empire, to be revived in the late eighteenth century. Hand-made lace was a popular fabric, and many veils became family heirlooms. Often the veil was the 'something borrowed' which every bride was obliged to have as part of her regalia. The veil worn by a bride whose marriage had been a happy one was thought to confer some of her good fortune on the new wearer. Traditionally, the bride arrives for the ceremony with the veil covering her face; the groom lifts it after the exchange of rings, signifying his acceptance of responsibility for his new wife.

The Garter

Often worn as the 'something blue' demanded by tradition for a bride's good fortune, the garter is usually thrown or raffled among the young single men at a modern wedding. In earlier centuries the newly-weds would be accompanied to their chamber by the entire wedding party, undressed, and put to bed amid much revelry. The stockings worn by both bride and groom were then tossed over the heads of their attendants to determine which of them would become the next to marry. The garter remains as a symbolic reminder of the ritual.

The Fan

Highly fashionable in Victorian times, the fan is a charming accessory for the bride. The manner in which a fan was held conveyed a message in the days when young ladies were strictly chaperoned, and the language of the fan was as important to their education as the language of flowers. The fan also served to display beautiful examples of hand-made lace and embroidery, often combined with fine inlays and carved motifs upon the handles.

The Bride's Shoes

Shoes are an ancient symbol of both fertility and authority. In some parts of Britain it was traditional for the bride's father to hand one of her shoes to the groom, who then tapped her on the head with it, signifying his acceptance of the transfer of authority over her between the two men. Guests would also throw shoes at the bride and groom, usually as they departed for their honeymoon; this has resulted in the more modern custom of tying old boots and tin cans to the bumper of their car.

Bride's headpiece with detachable long veil

Illustrated on page 25

Materials

2 No. 18 florist's stub wires, 35 mm long
3 No. 22 florist's stub wires, 35 mm long
white florist's tape
2.5 m white curling ribbon
6 sprays of crystal strings
16 embroidered leaves
8 white iridescent azaleas
3 white rosebuds
2 iridescent hyacinths with pearls
1 transparent plastic hair comb
3 m bridal tulle 274 cm wide (see note below)
white crochet cotton No. 40 or similar strong thread

Note The measurements given for the veil allow the longest section to reach the top of the lace trim at the hem of the wedding dress. The length of veil required should be calculated to fit the individual bride; more will be needed for a tall girl or a longer length.

1. Bind the two size 18 stub wires with white tape and set one aside while making the floral head-dress.

2. Make 7 bows from curling ribbon, each having 4 loops about 2 cm long. Secure the centres of the bows with a 10 cm length of No. 22 wire bent in half and twisted using pliers. Cover the wire with white tape.

3. Starting from one end with an embroidered leaf, bind the flowers, leaves and trimmings to one of the covered No. 18 wires using white tape and following the placement diagram.

4. Bend the finished trail into a gentle curve to fit over the head and adjust the flowers and leaves to hide the base wire.

5. Cut a piece of veiling 185 cm long and fold it in four with all the corners together. Fold the remaining veiling in half and place two corners on top of the first section, matching the straight and folded edges of both pieces. Cut away the corners with a gentle curve as shown in the diagram on page 11, using a large plate as a guide.

6. Open out the longer section of the veil and fold in two, 85 cm from one end. Keeping the shorter section uppermost, mark two points each 80 cm in from the edge. Gather the tulle between the marks to measure 20 cm and finish off the cotton securely. Sew the gathered

Placement diagram for bridal head-dress
(right-hand side only shown; to complete,
reverse sequence omitting
central rose).

Key

leaf (end)

crystal spray

azalea

leaf

crystal spray

leaf

azalea

leaf

leaf

leaf

hyacinth

rose (centre)

crystal spray

bow

azalea

bow

leaf

bow

rose

azalea

bow

leaf

Rounding the corners of the veiling

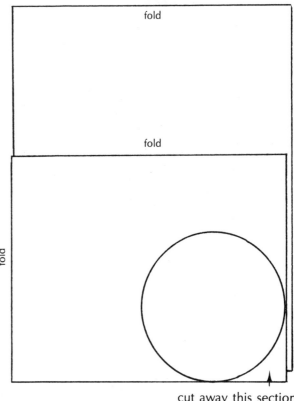

cut away this section
using plate as a guide
for the curve

section centrally to the flowered headband. Place the comb underneath the veil and sew it in place to the wire.

7. Fold over 1.5 cm on the straight edge of the remaining veil section and stitch to form a casing. Thread the second piece of covered No. 18 wire carefully through the casing and, using pliers, bend back each end of the wire to hold the tulle in place.

8. Make 4 buttonholed, crocheted or tatted loops from the strong thread and sew or knot them onto the covered wire at either end and 3 cm either side of the centre point. Thread loops can also be attached to the ends of the flower trail if necessary.

9. The long veil can be attached to the shorter section by inserting the teeth of the hair comb through the central loops. Bobby-pins pushed through the remaining loops secure the entire head-dress and, when required, the long section of veiling can be removed. The shortest length of tulle can be worn forward to cover the bride's face at the start of the ceremony.

Beaded Appliqué Dress Panels

Illustrated on pages 26–28

A plain gown can be made to look simply stunning with the addition of embroidered lace appliqués.

Lace is available by the metre or as separate motifs from all stockists of bridal fabrics. Motifs range from mirror-image pairs suitable for collars to large panels designed for use on a skirt or train. There are several styles of lace, including motifs with a corded edge, embroidered onto either tulle or organdie, in either white or ivory. Some motifs are already embroidered with pearl beads and sequins.

It is advisable to pin the pieces of lace for the bodice in place when fitting the dress, so that they are moulded to the curves of the body. Large panels can be slip-stitched directly to the dress by hand. A machine zigzag can often be used on a simple edging for a hem where the fabric lies flat.

If a large decorative panel needs to be built up from individual motifs, it is easiest to construct it onto a piece of tulle, either plain or embroidered, cut to the finished size and shape. Lay the motifs on top of the fabric and pin in place, taking care to match the centre lines of both the tulle foundation and the motifs. When satisfied with the layout, slip-stitch around each motif in turn to attach it to the net fabric. Small parts of the design can be cut from larger motifs to fill in gaps; provided each is anchored securely to the base fabric, this will present no problems. When the lace has been appliquéd to the net, the final bead embroidery can be done. Pick out features of the design such as flower centres with pearl beads or sequins; any beaded lace included in the design will prove a source of ideas for decorating the other motifs. Imagination is the only limit.

Pin the finished panel onto the dress and slip-stitch in place by hand. If the beading is very heavy and there is any tendency for it to sag, a further line of stitches worked around the largest motifs and through the dress fabric will help to support it.

The bodice of the dress, illustrated on page 27, features lace edging around the collar and shoulder seams. Part of the scalloped edge borders the back slit in the organza upper bodice and supports the pearl buttons and loops. The motifs are carried across the seam between the transparent organza and the white fabric. The main panel of lace on the bodice extends to just below the bust line and the gap above is filled with a narrow curved panel decorated with drop pearls, which inspired the treatment of the trim on the upper sleeves. Single motifs from the lace edging were used on the upper sleeve and cuffs. The complete edging appears at the hem of the gown.

The lace appliqué panel on the skirt consists of a small motif with two mirror-image motifs below it. The lace edging has been cut to form the border of the panel, and two small flowers, which were part of the curved panel on the bodice, fill in gaps at either side. The use of beads and sequins which match those on the purchased panel of beaded lace helps to coordinate the entire collection of separate motifs into one delightful whole.

Garter

Illustrated on page 37

Materials
2 m white satin ribbon, 25 mm wide
elastic, 17 mm wide, to fit leg measurement plus 2.5 cm
2 m white lace edging, 15 mm wide
20 cm blue silk ribbon, 7 mm wide
30 cm pale green silk ribbon, 3 mm wide
3 pearl beads, 3 mm diameter
matching sewing cotton

1. Cut the white ribbon into two pieces 1 m long and press 1 cm at each end to the wrong side. Pin the lace along the edges of one section of ribbon with the wrong sides uppermost and stitch in place. Pin the second piece of ribbon over the first with the wrong sides together and stitch along the sides, leaving the short edges open.

2. Thread the elastic through the ribbon casing, overlap the ends by 2.5 cm and stitch together firmly. Ease the ribbon ends together over the joined elastic and slip-stitch the edges of the ribbon together all round.

3. Make three ribbon flowers by cutting the blue ribbon into three pieces, joining the short ends of each piece together and gathering one long edge tightly. Fold the narrow green ribbon into loops about 2.5 cm long, and sew these over the join in the ribbon garter. Attach the blue flowers in a group on top of the loops, and finish by sewing a small pearl bead to the centre of each flower.

Smocked Fan

Illustrated on pages 6, 25

Materials

23 cm bamboo and paper fan
14 cm white satin, 115 cm wide
2.3 m white flat lace, 20 mm wide
50 cm gathered white lace, 30 mm wide
72 × 2 mm white pearl beads
DMC Stranded Cotton, 1 hank white
silk flowers and leaves
6 m white satin ribbon, 17 mm wide

1. Using a machine zigzag stitch, sew flat lace to each side of the strip of satin, covering the raw edges. Alternatively, the edges of the fabric can be overlocked and the lace sewn on top to cover the stitches.
2. Pleat 11 rows for smocking.
3. Following the chart, smock the pattern onto the fabric, threading a pearl bead onto each cable stitch marked X.
4. Gently part the paper from the end struts of the fan, taking care not to tear it. Fold the bamboo pieces out of the way while attaching the smocked panel.
5. Glue gathered lace edging to the top curve of the fan, pressing it down firmly into each fold of the paper.
6. Position the first smocked pleat against the left-hand edge of the paper and glue it in position, leaving the edge of the smocked panel overhanging.
7. Run a line of glue along the bottom curve of the paper and press the bottom of the smocked panel into it, distributing the gathers evenly.
8. Glue the right-hand edge of the smocked panel onto the paper with the last worked pleat lying in the last fold of the fan.

Smocking chart for smocked fan

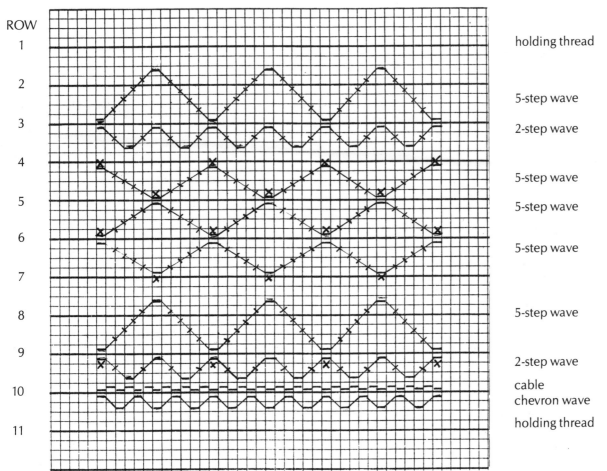

ROW	
1	holding thread
2	5-step wave
3	2-step wave
4	5-step wave
5	5-step wave
6	5-step wave
7	
8	5-step wave
9	2-step wave
10	cable / chevron wave
11	holding thread

Thread one bead on each cable stitch marked X

13

9. Fold the smocked panel gently downwards to expose the paper and run two lines of glue across the fan from side to side. Press the fabric lightly into this and glue the top edge in place across the curve of the fan so that the lace on the smocked panel just covers the base of the gathered lace frill.

10. Glue the right-hand end strut into place on the fan, aligning it with the edge of the embroidery. When the glue is dry, trim away any excess fabric which shows on the outside edge of the strut using a sharp craft knife.

11. Fold the left-hand edge of the smocking to the back of the fan. Glue it to the last panel of the paper. Trim the edge just inside the fold and glue the end strut of the bamboo back into place, covering the raw edges completely.

12. Make up a small spray of flowers and leaves and wire them in place at the base of the fan. Add a bow and trailing ribbons to cover the stems.

Beaded Shoe Clips

Illustrated on page 37

Materials
15 × 7.5 cm white felt
15 × 7.5 cm light coloured suede or leather
beading thread
2 shoe clips
beads: 2 × 4 mm pearls
    1 pack each of 2 mm pale green, 2 mm champagne pink, 2 mm gold, 2 mm iridescent white
Fray Stoppa

1. Transfer the heart pattern from the diagram twice onto the white felt, leaving 3 cm between the motifs.

2. Thread a beading needle with a doubled length of thread and knot the ends together. Fasten the thread with a back stitch through the felt at the dot in the centre of the first heart shape.

3. Commence beading by attaching one of the pearls over the marked dot. Surround this with a circle of champagne pink beads, then a second circle of gold beads. Fill the marked triangles with pale green beads.

4. Sew a line of champagne pink beads around the outside of the heart shape, then fill in the entire background area with iridescent white beads.

5. Complete the second heart shape to match, then turn the felt over and apply Fray Stoppa to the back of the beaded shapes, covering all the threads.

6. Trace the heart shape twice onto the leather. Open the shoe clips and position them over the dots on the hearts with the tongue sections pointing upwards. Sew the clips firmly in place onto the leather.

7. Cut around all the heart shapes leaving about 5 mm extra all round. Matching the centre dots on both sections, glue the leather hearts to the beaded ones with their wrong sides together. Leave to dry thoroughly, then trim the edges of the felt and leather to the outer edge of the beading on each heart.

Actual size trace pattern for beaded shoe clips

2
The Bridesmaids

Traditionally chosen from the bride's friends and sisters, the bridesmaids were dressed alike to confuse any evil spirits seeking to harm the bride. The superstition that a girl who is a bridesmaid three times will never see herself become a bride originates from the belief that she will have attracted too much bad luck.

Bridesmaid's Hair Comb

Illustrated on page 38

Materials
comb
No. 22 florist's stub wire, 35 cm long
white florist's tape

2 pearl loops
2 apricot azaleas
2 iridescent apricot orchids
1 small deep crimson rose

Key

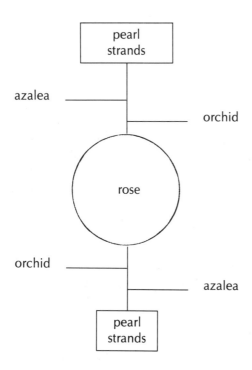

pearl strands

azalea

orchid

rose

orchid

azalea

pearl strands

1. Make up the flower spray following the diagram, taping the stems together with white florist's tape. Trim any excessively long wires to reduce the bulk.
2. Bind the stub wire along its entire length with white florist's tape. Use the covered wire to bind the floral spray onto the comb. Make sure that the wire ends are tucked neatly between the comb and the flowers.

Heart Hanger

Illustrated on page 38

Materials
heart-shaped wire frame, 16 cm long
white satin ribbons—50 cm × 10 mm; 1.4 m × 7 mm;
 1.2 m × 24 mm
60 cm × 24 mm white gathered lace edging
3 green rose leaves
3 small rosebuds
1 large rosebud
2 sprays small white flowers
green florist's tape

1. Fold the 10 mm wide ribbon in half lengthwise and slip-stitch the edges together, enclosing the wire heart shape.
2. Make up a spray of flowers following the placement diagram. Bind the stems completely with green florist's

tape then fold the end of the wires over 3 cm from the end to form a hook. Slot the top of the wire heart into this and secure the floral spray by binding the stem end to the back of the flower stems with florist's tape.
3. Cut a piece of 7 mm wide ribbon 80 cm long and tie the ends to the top of the heart over the flower stem to form a hanging loop. Make the 24 mm wide ribbon into a bow with 4 loops each 8 cm long, and tie the centre with the remainder of the 7 mm wide ribbon. Use the narrow ribbon to tie the bow in place around the top of the flower stems just beneath the heart-shaped frame, with a reef knot. Allow the ends to fall down the back of the heart hanger.
4. Complete the hanger by glueing the bound edge of the gathered lace around the edge of the frame on the back of the binding ribbon.

Flower placement diagram for heart hanger

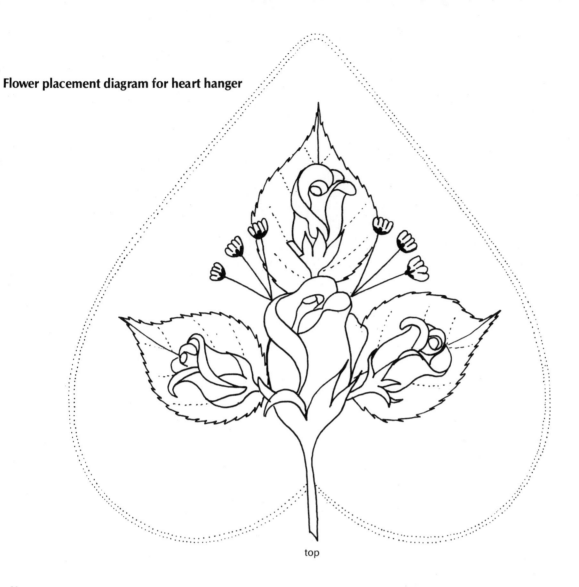

top

Key

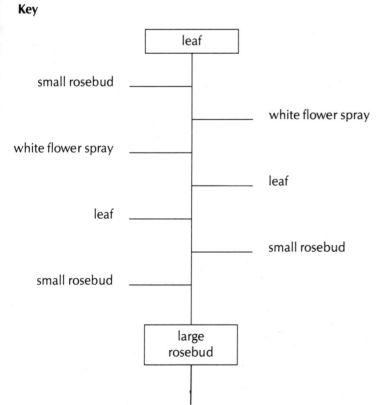

leaf

small rosebud

white flower spray

white flower spray

leaf

leaf

small rosebud

small rosebud

large
rosebud

17

Needlepoint Shoe Clips

Illustrated on page 37

Materials
15 × 7.5 cm plastic canvas, 10 holes per 2.5 cm
Madeira Glamour No. 8, 1 reel each of:
    gold 2424
    burgundy 2428
ribbon floss, 1 reel of iridescent white
15 × 7.5 cm white felt
2 shoe clips

1. Cut two shapes from the plastic canvas following the cutting diagram.
2. Following the chart, on which each line represents one thread of the canvas, stitch the design, starting with the central heart. Use 4 strands of thread for straight stitch and 2 for tent stitch and back stitch.
3. Oversew the edges of the shapes with gold thread doubled.
4. Cut the felt in half and sew one shoe clip to the centre of each section. Glue the felt pieces to the back of the needlepoint, wrong sides together, centring the shoe clips behind the hearts.
5. When the glue is completely dry, trim the excess felt from around the edges of the canvas.

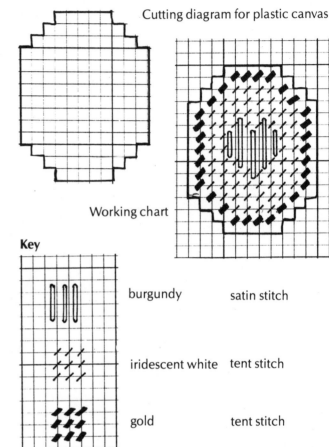

Cutting diagram for plastic canvas

Working chart

Key

burgundy	satin stitch
iridescent white	tent stitch
gold	tent stitch

Bridesmaid's Purse

Illustrated on page 39

Materials
40 × 20 cm fabric to match dress
1.2 m × 3 mm wide ribbon

1. Fold fabric in half, short sides together, to determine centre. Measure 9 cm either side of the fold and mark with a pin. Make two 1 cm buttonholes 5 mm either side of the pins, with the top of each 4 cm below the long edge of the fabric.
2. With right sides together, seam the short sides of the fabric.
3. Finish the raw edge on the long side nearest to the buttonholes with a narrow hem or overlock stitch.
4. Fold the top 3 cm to the wrong side of fabric and stitch in place to form a casing, with the buttonholes on the outside of the fabric.
5. With right sides together, match the seam to the centre point of the fabric on the remaining long edge and pin. Put a pin through the top of the folds at either end and bring them into the centre to meet next to the first pin, pleating the fabric. Stitch right across the folded fabric, through all layers, 1 cm from the edge.
6. Cut the length of ribbon in half and thread one piece through the casing, passing in and out of each buttonhole in turn. Knot the ends together. Repeat with the second length of ribbon, starting at the opposite pair of buttonholes. A bead can be threaded onto each ribbon loop to cover the knot if desired.

Marking buttonholes and top casing for bridesmaid's purse

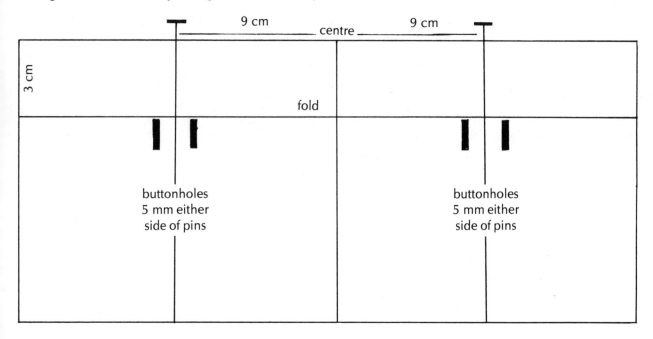

Folding and pleating the fabric for the bridesmaid's purse

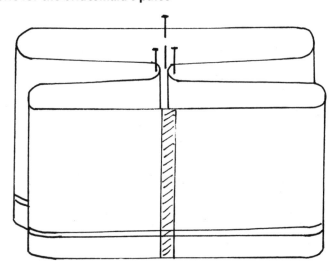

Embroidered Handkerchiefs

Illustrated on page 39

Materials
pure cotton or linen handkerchief with lace edging
DMC Stranded Cotton, 1 hank each of:
    dark pink 223
    pale pink 225
    green 523
    blue 825
Madeira art. 9803, 1 packet gold 3004

Fray Stoppa
Perfect Sew fabric stabiliser

Note: The hankerchief can be purchased, or you can make your own from a 20 cm square of batiste or voile. Round the corners of the square slightly and finish the edges with a rolled or overlocked narrow hem. Slip-stitch lace around the edges to cover the hem-stitching or stiffen the whole piece with fabric stabiliser and machine embroider a scalloped edge. Treat the back of the embroidery with Fray Stoppa, following the manufacturer's instructions, and carefully cut away the excess fabric when dry.

1. Cover an area approximately 7 cm square in one corner of the handkerchief with Perfect Sew, following the instructions on the bottle, and allow the fabric to dry.
2. Use a fade-out pen to trace the chosen pattern from the diagram directly onto the stabilised corner of the fabric.
3. Follow the stitch placement diagram to embroider the motif, using 2 strands of cotton throughout. Work the gold heart last, using 2 strands of the metallic thread.
4. Turn embroidery over and treat with Fray Stoppa. Allow to dry, then wash gently in cool running water to remove the fabric stabiliser and any remaining pattern markings. Press lightly with a damp cloth on the reverse side of the fabric.

Stitch diagrams for embroidered handkerchiefs

Key

green	523	stem stitch
green	523	lazy daisy stitch
dark pink	223	bullion stitch (centre)
pale pink	225	bullion stitch (outer petals)
gold	3004	back stitch

Key

green	523	stem stitch
green	523	lazy daisy stitch
dark pink	223	bullion stitch (centre)
pale pink	225	bullion stitch (outer petals)
blue	825	back stitch
gold	3004	chain stitch

Actual size trace patterns for embroidered handkerchiefs

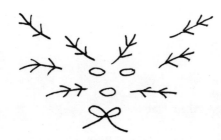

3
The Ceremony

The Ring

A traditional symbol of eternity, the unbroken circle of a ring has been the symbol of a lasting contract for many centuries. The theory promoted in Roman times that a vein in the third finger of the left hand flowed to the heart led to the custom of placing the wedding or betrothal ring on that finger. The tradition varies widely, however, with rings having been worn on the right hand and even on the thumb. Rings have been made of many metals, from iron to gold, and in many styles. The 'gimmal ring' consisted of three bands fastened together with a pair of clasped hands. These were separated on the betrothal of a couple, with each partner and a witness taking a separate ring until the marriage ceremony, at which the whole thing was brought together once more. Victorian brides often had precious stones set into their rings, with each gemstone representing a particular quality. Sometimes the initial letters of the group of stones would spell a name, or a short word such as 'love'. Engraved bands were popular choices also. In earlier times the inscription was made on the outside of the ring, but in modern times it is more usual for it to appear on the inside. Superstition has it that dropping the ring will cause disaster, particularly for the groom, and partly because of this the best man now assumes responsibility for the ring until it is needed during the ceremony. A more recent trend is to have the rings for both bride and groom tied in place on a special ring pillow which is carried by a small pageboy or bridesmaid.

Bridal Favours

Now most often the term used for the good luck charms given to the bride after the ceremony by the guests, the bridal favour was originally part of the wedding regalia, when the groom and his men would wear a knot of ribbons in colours which matched the bride's gown. The bridesmaids would hand similar tokens to the guests as they left the church. At Greek weddings small boxes of sugared almonds are usually given to the female guests after the ceremony in a similar custom. Bridal favours have varied from ribbons to flowers and even scented gloves in times past.

Horseshoes

The horseshoe has always been a symbol of good luck provided, in English custom, that it is hung with the ends uppermost 'so that the luck will not run out'. In Australia however, this custom is not always observed, and it is more usual for the horseshoe to be held upside-down.

Bells

The belief that evil spirits, ever watchful for a chance to cause harm to the newlyweds, needed to be frightened away from the ceremony resulted in the tradition of guests making as much noise as possible with all manner of instruments. The peal of church bells is an extension of this custom, and serves to publicise to all within earshot that a wedding has taken place. The ringers themselves are only too happy to have the chance to display their skills; the marriage of one of their own members is a special cause for celebration, when a new peal may be composed and rung especially for the event.

Ring Pillow

Illustrated on page 39

Materials
30 cm square cotton voile
26 × 60 cm pink satin
60 cm × 12 mm pink silk ribbon
DMC Stranded Cotton, 1 hank white
Madeira art. 9803, 1 packet gold 3004
Madeira Glamour No. 8, 1 reel gold 2424
Perfect Sew fabric stabiliser
1 m × 20 mm white lace insertion
1 m × 50 mm gathered lace edging
60 cm × 3 mm white ribbon
soft toy filling

1. Prepare the voile by saturing it with fabric stabiliser following the manufacturer's instructions. Allow to dry then iron flat.
2. Use fade-out pen to trace the pattern from the full-size diagram onto the centre of the fabric, then mount it in an embroidery hoop to work.
3. Following the stitch placement diagram and using three strands of white cotton, embroider the pattern. Take care to work the ends of the threads into the back of previous stitches when starting and finishing, and carry thread from one line to the next by taking tiny running stitches along the outer line, where they will be covered by stem stitch worked around the edge of each shape. Use 4 strands of gold thread to work bands of chain stitch across each bell, then fill in each of the hanging ribbons by working 3 long straight stitches from the bottom of the bow to the top of the bell using Glamour thread. Sew satin stitch over these lines in the same thread.
4. Fold one end of the pink silk ribbon diagonally to match the line marked A on the pattern, and using matching sewing thread slip-stitch it in place. Continue stitching along the side to attach the ribbon to the bottom curve of the design. Fold and tuck the ribbon under itself to accommodate the curve of the bell, then continue to stitch the edge to the pattern line right up to the knot.

Twist and fold the ribbon to follow the line of the first loop, and continue to sew the edge to the pattern line as far as point B.
5. Fold the ribbon over at point B and stitch the fold along the outer line of the shape. Stitch the straight edge to point C, then fold the ribbon underneath and stitch through the folded edge to D, and down the straight edge back into the knot area.
6. Repeat these steps to sew the ribbon to the outer edges of the second loop, then twist it and take it out to the end of the second ribbon at E, pleating and tucking to match the curve around the second bell. Trim excess ribbon 5 mm beyond the edge and tuck in this seam allowance when finishing the end.
7. Slip-stitch the remaining ribbon edges in place, gathering them to fit the curves, and creasing the folds as they enter the area of the knot.
8. Cut a 6 cm piece of ribbon and fold in half, raw edges together. Sew the folded edge to the top of the knot area, tucking in the corners to achieve a rounded shape, then sew down one side. Tuck the excess fabric under, rounding bottom corners to match, and secure bottom edge in place. Sew the second side of the knot and finish off.
9. Pin lace insertion around the square marked with a dotted line on the pattern, mitring the corners. Slip-stitch to the voile along the inner edge. Stitch the folded edges of the corners through the lace edging only.
10. Place embroidery face up on a smooth surface and carefully cut away the voile, leaving 5 mm projecting beyond the edge of the lace all round. Turn this seam allowance to the inside and slip-stitch it to the outer edge of the lace.
11. Slip-stitch the bound edge of the lace edging to the back of the finished square, mitring the corners and joining the raw edges as neatly and invisibly as possible.
12. Wash the embroidered square gently to remove the fabric stabiliser and any remaining pattern markings, then dry and press lightly on the wrong side.

Actual size trace pattern for ring pillow

See next page for stitch placement diagram

13. Fold the pink fabric in half, right sides together, and seam the long edges. Turn to the right side and press. Measure 23 cm from the fold and turn the excess fabric to the inside. Press creases, then trim the surplus fabric to leave 2.5 cm turnings.

14. Stuff the cushion with fibre toy filling and slip-stitch the folded edges together.

15. Pin the finished embroidery over the pillow, matching the outer edge of the lace insertion to the seams and fold. Slip-stitch the panel to the top of the cushion.

16. Cut white ribbon in two and fold each piece in half to determine the centre. Sew through the creases to attach each of them to the marked points at the bottom of the bells. The rings are threaded onto these ribbons, which are then tied in bows.

Stitch placement diagram for ring pillow **Key**

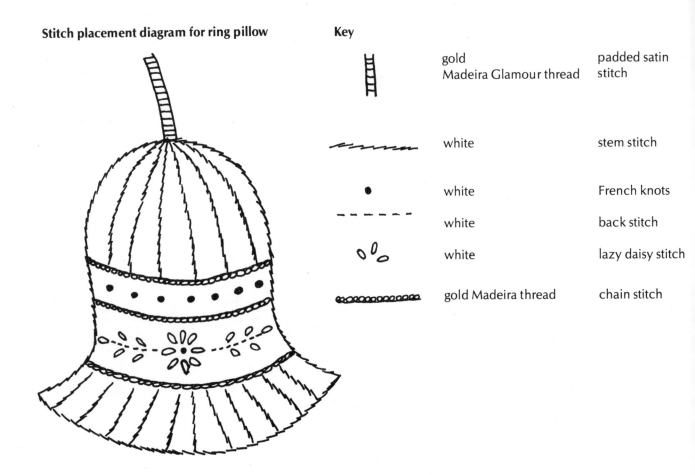

	gold Madeira Glamour thread	padded satin stitch
	white	stem stitch
	white	French knots
	white	back stitch
	white	lazy daisy stitch
	gold Madeira thread	chain stitch

Embroidered Horseshoe Favour

Illustrated on page 40

Materials
40 × 20 cm white satin
30 × 15 cm white card
70 cm × 15 mm wide white gathered lace edging
1.5 m × 7 mm white satin ribbon
15 cm square wadding
DMC Stranded Cotton, 1 hank each of:
   ecru
   dark rose 223
   pale green 524
   pink 3354
2 white embroidered leaves
1 iridescent white azalea flower

1. Cut the satin into two 20 cm square pieces. Trace the full size design onto one section, then embroider the details following the stitch diagram, using three strands of cotton throughout. Note that the heart shapes are drawn twice; use the shaded ones if you prefer to hang the horseshoe with the curve at the bottom in the English fashion.

2. Trace the shape twice onto the white card and cut out. Cover one shape with the plain satin square, trimming it to shape and glueing turnings onto the wrong side.

3. Glue wadding lightly to one side of the second card shape. Cover this with the embroidered satin, centring the design over the shape. Trim to fit the cardboard shape, leaving 1 cm turnings, and glue these firmly over the back of the card.

4. Glue the bound edge of the gathered lace around the shape on the back of the embroidered section.

5. Cut a 95 cm length of ribbon and fold in half. Glue the ends to the wrong side of the plain satin covered card at the top of the shape. Glue both sections of card

Wedding dress with beaded appliqué lace panels and neckline (page 12), set off by a flowered headpiece with detachable long veil (page 9) and a dainty smocked fan (page 13)

Details of the front and back necklines of the beaded wedding dress

26

Detail of the bodice front of the wedding dress

Detail of beaded lace panel on the front skirt of the wedding dress

Detail of the beaded lace motif on the upper sleeve

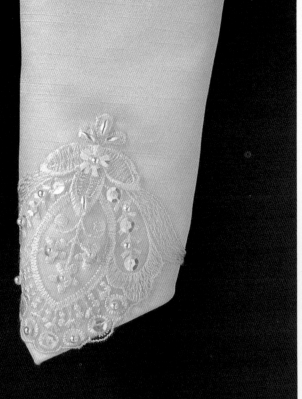

Detail of the beaded lace motif at the wrist

together and weigh down with a few books while the glue dries.

6. Make a small floral spray using the iridescent azalea and the embroidered leaves, and tie the stem with a bow made from the remaining ribbon. Trim the stem ends to about 2 cm and glue the spray in place at the top of the shape in front of the hanging ribbon.

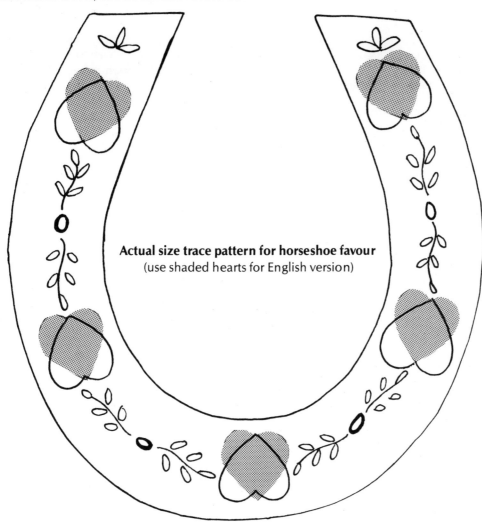

Actual size trace pattern for horseshoe favour
(use shaded hearts for English version)

Stitch placement diagram for horseshoe favour

Key

lazy daisy	green	524	lazy daisy stitch
stem	green	524	stem stitch
rose	dark rose	223	bullion stitch (centres)
	pink	3354	bullion stitch (outer petals)
satin	ecru		satin stitch

29

Lace Bell Bridal Favour

Illustrated on page 40

Materials

20 × 40 cm white satin
15 cm square white lace fabric
60 cm × 15 mm white gathered lace edging
60 cm pearl string
1 × 20 mm drop pearl bead
15 × 30 cm white card
2 small green leaves
1 small burgundy rosebud
40 cm burgundy curling ribbon
1 m × 7 mm wide white satin ribbon
15 cm square wadding

1. Cut the piece of satin into two 20 cm squares. Trace the bell shape twice onto white card and cut out. Cover one shape with white satin and set aside.
2. Lightly glue the wadding to one side of the other bell shape and trim away the excess. Cover the wadding with the second piece of satin, then the all-over lace fabric. Glue the turnings securely to the wrong side.

3. Glue the bound edge of the gathered lace around the back edges of the lace-covered shape.
4. Fold the narrow ribbon in half and glue the ends to the wrong side of the plain satin-covered bell shape at the top.
5. Glue the two covered shapes together and weigh down while the glue dries.
6. Finish the favour by glueing a strip of lace with the bound edge on the line marked across the bell. Glue the pearl string on top of the binding of the lace and around the edge of the lace bell shape. Glue the 20 mm pearl bead to the spot marked for the clapper.
7. Make a small flower spray using the green leaves and the rosebud. Trim the stem ends to about 2 cm. Make the burgundy curling ribbon into a small 4-looped bow and wire this in with the leaves and bud. Fold over the stem ends and tuck behind the flower before glueing the spray in place at the top of the bell in front of the hanging ribbon.

Actual size trace pattern for lace bell bridal favour

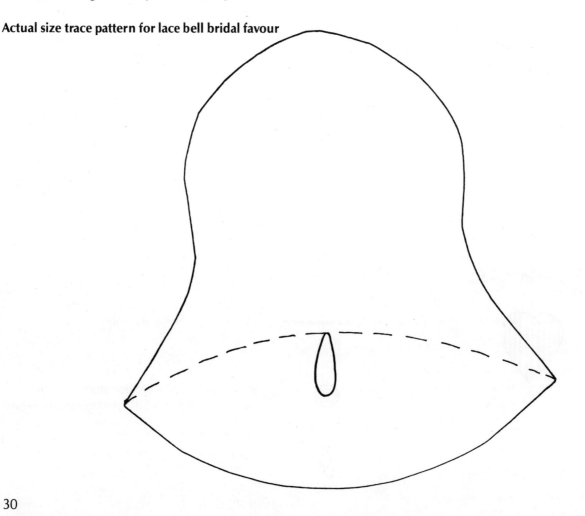

Scented Ribbon-weave Bridal Favour

Illustrated on page 40

Materials

1 m white ribbon 7 mm wide
70 cm gathered lace 25 mm wide
20 cm square scrap of voile
potpourri
scrap thin white card
small silk and pearl flowers, embroidered leaves
white florist's tape
craft glue
70 cm narrow white braid
70 cm pearl string or satin cord
for the ribbon weaving—4 m white ribbon 13 mm wide;
   20 cm square iron-on interfacing

1. Prepare the ribbon weaving following the general directions in Chapter 7, using the 13 mm wide ribbon cut into 16 cm lengths. Trace the heart shape from the pattern diagram onto a piece of thin white card twice and cut out. Use one card shape to trace the outline on the back of the ribbon weaving and machine stitch inside this line as directed in the general instructions.

2. Coat one side of one card shape with glue and while it is still tacky press it into the potpourri. Make sure that the card is completely covered. Place the shape, potpourri side down, on top of the piece of voile and, cutting and snipping the fabric where necessary, glue the turnings down over the back of the shape, enclosing the potpourri completely.

3. Cut an 85 cm length of narrow ribbon, fold it in half, and glue the ends to the back of the shape at the top to form a long hanging loop. Glue the gathered lace edging around the edge of the shape on the back and set aside to allow the glue to dry.

4. Cut out the prepared ribbon weaving just outside the stitching line and glue it to the second card shape.

5. Glue the ribbon-covered shape on top of the potpourri-filled shape, enclosing the lace edging between them. Trim the edges of the potpourri-covered shape with a length of narrow braid glued in place, then trim the front of the shape in the same way, using satin cording or pearl string. Start and finish the trimming at the point nearest to the hanging loop.

6. Make up a small spray of flowers and leaves, binding the stems together with white florist's tape. Tie a ribbon bow around the stem, trim the wires to about 2 cm, and glue the flowers in place on the completed favour.

Actual size trace pattern for scented ribbon-weave bridal favour

Pew or Table Decoration

Illustrated on page 40

Materials

wire bell shape, 20 cm high
2 m × 10 mm white satin ribbon
60 cm × 35 mm burgundy satin ribbon
1 size 20 stub wire, 35 cm long
white florist's tape
6 white embroidered leaves
3 crystal sprays
1 pearl loop spray
4 white azaleas
1 iridescent white azalea
2 iridescent hyacinths with pearl stamens
15 cm burgundy curling ribbon

1. Starting at the centre top, bind the wire bell shape with the 10 mm wide satin ribbon, covering it completely. Secure the ends with a small dab of glue.
2. Make up the floral spray following the placement diagram and bind the stems with white florist's tape.
3. Fold the stub wire in half and slip it through the top of the bell shape with the ends pointing upwards. With white florist's tape bind the wires together from top to bottom, and tape over the point where the loop meets the bell.
4. Tape the ends of the floral spray securely to the wire, positioning the flowers just below the top of the bell. Make a two-loop bow from the burgundy ribbon, tying the centre with a length of matching curling ribbon. Trim the ends of the ribbon in an inverted V shape, then tie the bow onto the stub wire just above the flowers. Knot the ends of the ribbon and trim off the excess.
5. To fix the decoration in place, bend the end of the stub wire over to make a hook. This can either be attached directly to the top of the pew or hooked over a length of ribbon tied around the pew end. The bell can also be used as a decoration on the front of the bridal table or the cake stand.

Key

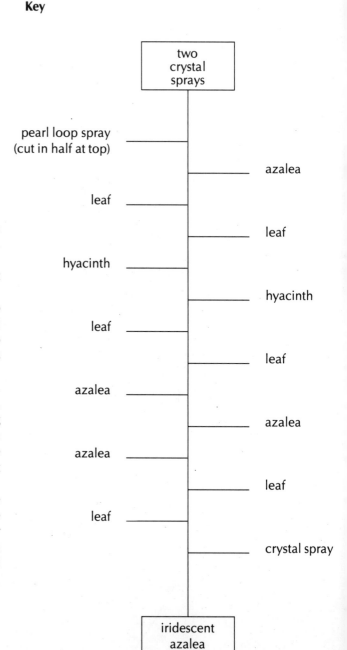

two crystal sprays

pearl loop spray (cut in half at top)

azalea

leaf

leaf

hyacinth

hyacinth

leaf

leaf

azalea

azalea

azalea

leaf

leaf

crystal spray

iridescent azalea

top

Flower placement diagram for pew decoration

4
The Reception

Bonbonnière
A charming custom which is being adopted by many Australians is the giving of bonbonnières to the women attending a wedding. Depending on the origins of the bride's family, they can contain either all white or a mixture of coloured sugared almonds; the containers in some cases are extremely elaborate and costly. Almonds are a traditional symbol of fertility, and often a less elaborate bonbonnière will contain just five of them, each signifying a different blessing for the happy couple.

The Wedding Cake
The importance of cake at a wedding feast has endured through many thousands of years and most cultures. Roman brides were crowned with crumbs to ensure their fertility, and small cakes were commonly thrown among guests in mediaeval times. Three hundred years ago separate cakes were made for the bride and groom. The bride's cake was a light one, while the groom's was a rich fruit cake. In Victorian times the groom's cake was often presented to the guests in small packages to take home with them, and the belief arose that a single girl who placed her slice of cake beneath her pillow would that night dream of the man she would marry. In modern times it is usual for the cake to be made in several tiers. The top one is traditionally reserved for the bride and groom to keep and cut either on their first anniversary or at the christening of their first child.

Smocked Basket Liner

Illustrated on page 49

Materials
30 cm white satin 115 cm wide
DMC Stranded Cotton, 1 skein each of:
   white
   pale green 369
   dark apricot 754
   pale apricot 948

2.6 m flat white lace, 15 mm wide
20 cm diameter flower basket
1.2 m gathered lace edging 20 mm wide
60 cm white satin bias binding 25 mm wide
60 cm white lace insertion, 14 mm wide
60 cm apricot ribbon 7 mm wide
9 cm diameter circle white card

34

12 cm diameter circle white satin
9 cm diameter circle wadding
2 m ribbon 7 mm wide for trimming

1. Turn under 1 cm at the end of the bias binding and, starting at one side of the basket, fold the strip lengthways to fully enclose the handle, slip-stitching the long folded edges together on the outside. Cut away excess binding at the other end of the handle and turn under 1 cm to match the first side.
2. Cut the strip of lace edging in half and slip-stitch the two pieces together along their bound edges. Open the completed strip out to lie flat. Pin over the basket handle, covering the seam of the bias binding.
3. Thread lace insertion with 7 mm wide apricot ribbon and pin on top of the gathered lace strip. Slip-stitch all layers together firmly and remove the pins. Trim off the excess lace and ribbon level with the bottom of the basket handle.
4. Cut two 10 cm wide strips from the satin across the width of the fabric. With right sides facing, join the two pieces together along one short side with a narrow seam. Finish the raw edges either with a machine zigzag stitch or by overlocking. Sew flat lace over one edge only, covering the stitching.

5. Pleat 7 rows in preparation for smocking. Following the chart, smock the pattern between the holding rows in white and add grub roses in apricot shades with green leaves in the centre of each large shape as shown.
6. Match the pattern at the remaining short edges and sew together as invisibly as possible. Trim any excess fabric, leaving a seam allowance of 1.5 cm. Withdraw the pleating threads.
7. Apply glue to the top inside edge of the basket and press the outer edge of the smocked satin onto it. Distribute the gathers evenly around the basket, with the two seams at each side next to the ends of the handle.
8. Rolling the smocking back, place glue around the base of the basket, then press the inner edge of the smocked circle into place, keeping it as flat and even as possible.
9. Glue the circle of wadding on top of the white card. Gather the edge of the circle of white satin and use it to cover the wadding and the card. Pull up the gathers tightly and fasten off the thread securely.
10. Glue or slip-stitch the satin-covered circle to the centre of the basket, covering the raw edges of the smocking.
11. Use remaining lengths of ribbon to trim the base of the basket handle on each side with bows and trailing ribbons.

Smocking chart for smocked basket liner

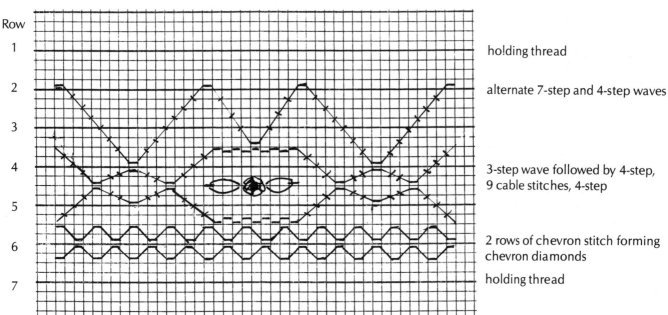

Row	
1	holding thread
2	alternate 7-step and 4-step waves
3	
4	3-step wave followed by 4-step, 9 cable stitches, 4-step
5	
6	2 rows of chevron stitch forming chevron diamonds
7	holding thread

Embroider centre of cable boxes with grub roses:

⌒	pale green	369	lazy daisy stitch
✦	dark apricot	754	bullion stitch (centre)
✿	pale apricot	948	bullion stitch (outer petals)

Corsage Bonbonnière

Illustrated on page 49

Materials
5 sugared almonds
5 nylon-covered leaves
3 embroidered white leaves
2 iridescent azaleas
40 cm curling ribbon
10 cm No. 18 stub wire
white florist's tape

1. Following the placement diagram, wire the leaves and flowers together, starting with the first nylon-covered leaf. Bind in each element of the spray in turn using the white florist's tape.
2. Make a six-loop bow from the curling ribbon. Wire the centre of the loops and place the bow at the base of the floral spray. Tape it to the flower stems.
3. Trim all stems 2.5 cm below the bow and cover the wires completely with white tape, making sure that there are no sharp wire ends.
4. Fold the nylon-covered leaves in half lengthways and insert a sugared almond into each one.

Flower placement diagram for corsage bonbonnière

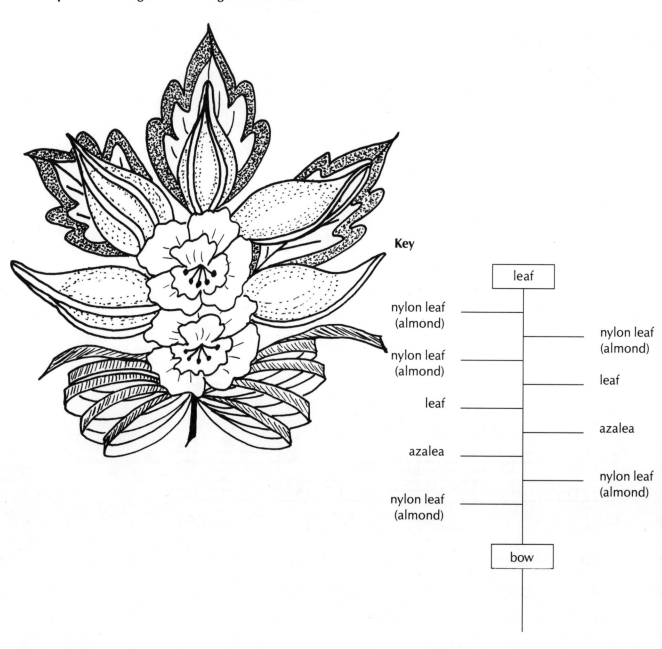

Key

leaf

nylon leaf (almond)

nylon leaf (almond)

leaf

azalea

nylon leaf (almond)

nylon leaf (almond)

leaf

azalea

nylon leaf (almond)

bow

Satin garter trimmed with lace and ribbon flowers (page 12)

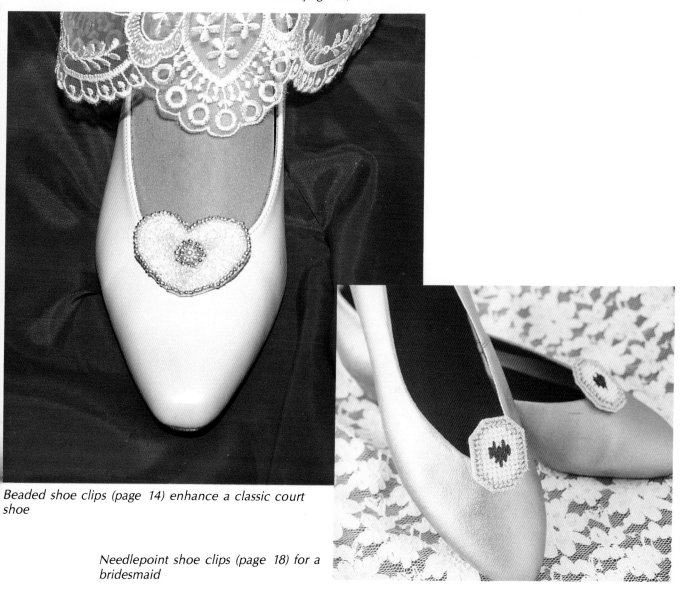

Beaded shoe clips (page 14) enhance a classic court shoe

Needlepoint shoe clips (page 18) for a bridesmaid

Dainty floral hair comb for a bridesmaid (page 15)

Heart hanger filled with flowers (page 16) to be carried by a bridesmaid

Bridesmaid's purse (page 18) and delicately embroidered handkerchiefs (page 19)

Ring pillow (page 22)

Three bridal favours from pages 24, 30 and 31

Pew or table decoration (page 32)

Heart Bonbonnière

Illustrated on page 49

Materials
5 sugared almonds
14 × 22 cm bridal tulle
5 pieces No. 22 stub wire, 17.5 cm long
white florist's tape
2 green flocked velvet leaves
2 pink ribbon roses
12 cm square burgundy fabric
12 cm square gold paper
12 × 24 cm white card
35 cm white curling ribbon
35 cm × 15 mm white gathered lace edging

1. Trace the heart pattern twice onto the white card and cut out.
2. Cover one piece of card with gold paper and set aside.
3. Cover the second piece of card with the burgundy fabric, glueing the turnings to the wrong side of the shape. Glue the lace edging to the back of the fabric-covered card, starting at the centre top.

4. Cut 5 circles each 6.5 cm in diameter from the bridal tulle. Place an almond in the centre of each and gather the edges to enclose it completely. Bind the gathered edges with white sewing cotton to form a short stem.
5. Double the 17.5 cm lengths of wire and thread one through the base of each tulle-covered almond. Tape the wires to the tulle with florist's tape, and continue taping to the end of each stem.
6. Wire the almonds into a small spray with the leaves and flowers, following the placement diagram. Trim the stems and cover them completely with florist's tape. Make a 4-loop bow of white curling ribbon and wire it to the top of the spray as shown.
7. Assemble the bonbonnière by glueing the two covered shapes together with wrong sides facing. Weigh them down with a couple of books while the glue dries. Glue the flower spray onto the heart shape with the leaves underneath, making sure that the glue does not come in contact with the almonds.

Actual size trace pattern for heart bonbonnière

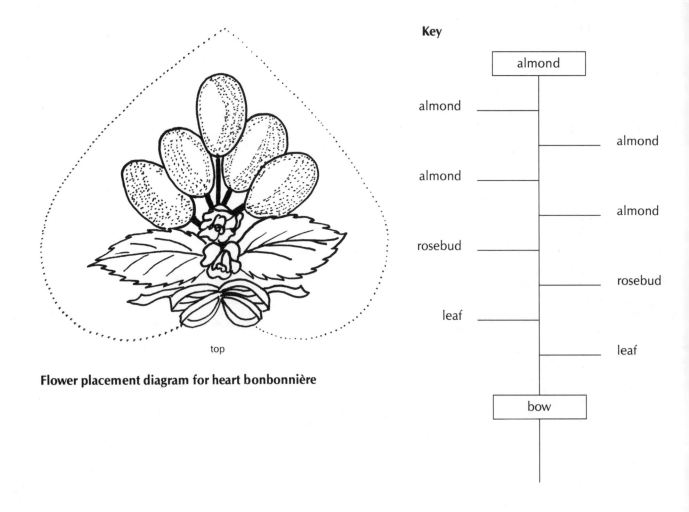

Key

almond

almond — almond

almond — almond

rosebud — rosebud

leaf — leaf

bow

Flower placement diagram for heart bonbonnière

top

Cross-stitch Greetings Card

Illustrated on page 50

Materials
10 × 15 cm white Aida fabric, 14 holes per inch
DMC Stranded Cotton, 1 hank each of:
    medium rose pink 223
    dark rose pink 315
    dark blue 791
    French blue 793
    sky blue 799
    light blue 800
    dark green 936
    light green 3052
    light rose pink 3354
    pale pink 3713
apricot coloured card blank, 15 × 10.5 cm,
    with 9 × 6 cm rectangular cut-out
9 × 6 cm thin wadding

1. Embroider the design onto the Aida fabric using the colours and stitches shown on the chart. Use three strands of cotton for all embroidery.
2. Fold the card so that the right-hand flap is underneath the cut-out window, and glue the wadding lightly to the centre of the card so that it is framed by the cut-out. Glue the cross-stitched panel to the back of the window, centring the vertical band of the design and making sure that no unworked fabric shows at the top of the band.
3. Glue the card flap in place beneath the embroidery, and place under a couple of heavy books until the glue dries.

Working chart for cross-stitch greetings card
(each square on the chart represents one stitch)

centre

centre

medium rose pink	223
dark rose pink	315
dark blue	791
French blue	793
sky blue	799
light blue	800
dark green	936
light green	3052
light rose pink	3354
pale pink	3713

Heart and Bells Card

Illustrated on page 50

Materials
gold bell cake decoration
30 cm × 2 mm burgundy satin ribbon
11 cm square apricot silky-look fabric
30 cm pearl string
30 cm × 17 mm white gathered lace edging
11 cm square wadding
white card blank, 15.5 × 11 cm with 7 cm heart cut-out

1. Cut the wadding to fit into the heart-shaped cut-out, and glue it lightly to the inside flap of the card so that it shows through the window.

2. Glue the silky fabric to the back of the cut-out heart on the card, then glue the backing panel in place so that the wadding is placed beneath the heart.

3. Trim the edge of the heart shape with gathered lace, easing it slightly around the curved edges of the heart so that it lies flat. Glue the pearl string over the bound edge of the lace.

4. Thread the narrow ribbon through the holes at the top of the bell motif and tie it in a bow. Using scissors or a sharp craft knife, cut off the shank at the back of the bells, then glue the motif in place at the centre of the padded heart. Trim the ribbon ends to the same length.

Découpage Card

Illustrated on page 64

Materials
15.5 × 10.5 cm white card blank
scraps of lace or lace edging
reproduction Victorian scrap picture

1. If the card has a window cut-out, glue the right-hand flap to the inside of the card, covering the back of it.

2. Cut all the white background areas away from the scrap picture and glue it in the centre of the front of the card.

3. Arrange the lace to form a frame around the scrap picture. When satisfied with the arrangement, glue the lace in place.

Beaded Perforated Paper Card

Illustrated on page 50

Materials
11 cm square white perforated paper
1 reel gold ribbon floss
3 × 22 mm long gold leaf-shaped sequins
Beads—3 × 2 mm gold; 18 × 2 mm pink;
   28 × 1.5 mm green
apricot-coloured card blank, 15.5 × 10.5 cm with
   7 cm heart cut-out
30 cm × 17 mm white gathered lace edging
beading thread

1. Following the chart, on which each line represents one grid of the perforated paper, embroider the lettering in back stitch using gold ribbon floss.

2. Thread a beading needle with a doubled length of thread and knot the ends together. Attach the beads as shown on the chart, using beaded tent stitch.

3. Attach the leaf-shaped sequins in the positions shown on the chart, with one stitch through each of the holes at the ends of each leaf.

4. Glue the perforated paper embroidery centrally behind the cut-out heart on the card, then glue the right-hand flap of the card over it to cover the back of the work.

5. Glue lace edging around the heart on the front of the card, easing it to fit around the curves so that it will lie flat. Glue a length of gold ribbon floss around the shape to cover the bound edge of the lace. Cut a piece of ribbon floss 25 cm long and tie it into a small bow about 4.5 cm across. Trim the ends and glue the bow in place at the bottom point of the heart shape.

Working chart for beaded perforated paper card
(the lines on the chart represent the grid of the paper)

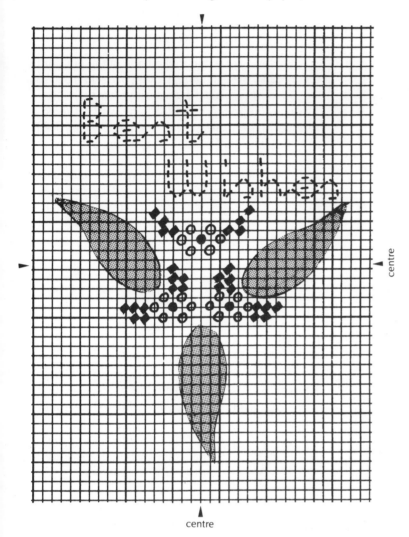

centre

centre

Key

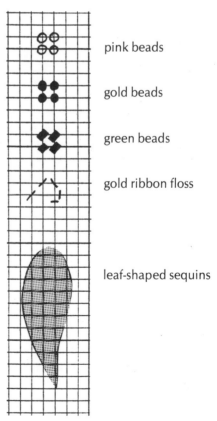

pink beads

gold beads

green beads

gold ribbon floss

leaf-shaped sequins

Guest Book

Illustrated on page 51

Materials
guest book, 22 × 18 cm
30 × 115 cm burgundy silk fabric
22 × 18 cm white perforated paper
ribbon floss, 1 reel of gold
DMC Stranded Cotton, 1 hank each of:
    light rose 223
    dark rose 315
    pale apricot 819
    dark green 936
    light green 3052
    bright pink 3354
    pale pink 3713
    white
small angel head (optional)
white card, 18 × 42 cm

1. Cut a piece of silk fabric 53 × 27 cm and place the guest book, opened, on the wrong side of the fabric. Clip the material either side of the spine and trim off a small piece between the cuts, leaving approximately 1.5 cm to turn over into the spine. Glue the fabric in place all round the outer edges of the cover, taking care to leave enough 'give' in the fabric to allow the book to close properly.
2. Cut 2 pieces of thin card 17.5 × 21 cm and cover each of them with a rectangle of the remaining fabric. Glue them inside the back and front covers of the book, covering the raw edges of the material. Set the book aside while preparing the embroidered panel.
3. Using two strands of white cotton for all embroidery and following the chart, on which each line represents one grid of the perforated paper, stitch the border pattern. Start with the outer row of cross stitch, then work the fan-shaped straight stitch groups. Finish with the triple-size cross stitches and the back-stitched details. (Note that the inner cross-stitch border appears again on the chart for the centre motif of the guest book.)
4. Change to the second chart and work the rose design using two strands of cotton throughout. Note that on this chart each square represents one stitch; the border duplicates the inner row of cross stitches from the border chart and is only shown to help with correct positioning of the main motif.
5. Work the lettering in a single strand of gold ribbon floss.
6. When the embroidery is complete, carefully cut around the edge with a small pair of sharp-pointed embroidery scissors, leaving 2 mm of paper outside the stitching.

7. Lightly smear the back of the border area of the panel with glue, and position it centrally on the front cover of the guest book. Weigh down with a couple of books while the glue dries.
8. Glue the small angel-head, if used, centrally in the gap at the top of the flower wreath design.

Key

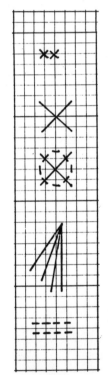

cross stitch

triple-size cross stitch

back stitch worked over the arms of triple-size cross stitches

straight stitch

back stitch

All stitching is in DMC white stranded cotton.

Working chart for outer border of guest book cover
(each line on the chart represents one grid of the perforated paper;
one quarter of the entire design is shown)

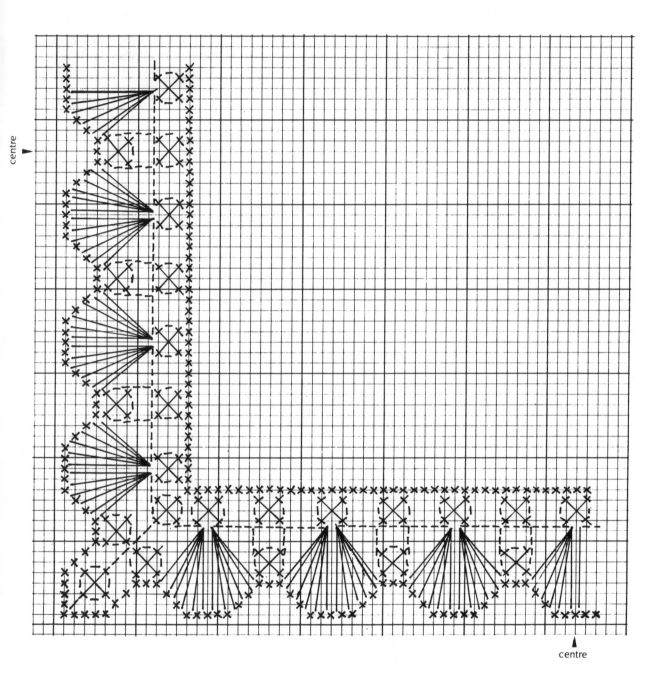

Working chart for centre panel of guest book
(each square on the chart represents one stitch)

centre

centre

centre

Key appears on page 53

Delicately smocked basket liner (page 34)

Corsage bonbonnière (page 36)

Heart bonbonnière (page 41)

Cross-stitch greetings card (page 42)

Beaded perforated paper card (page 44)

Heart and bells card (page 44)

50

Embroidered perforated paper panel enhances a guest book (page 46)

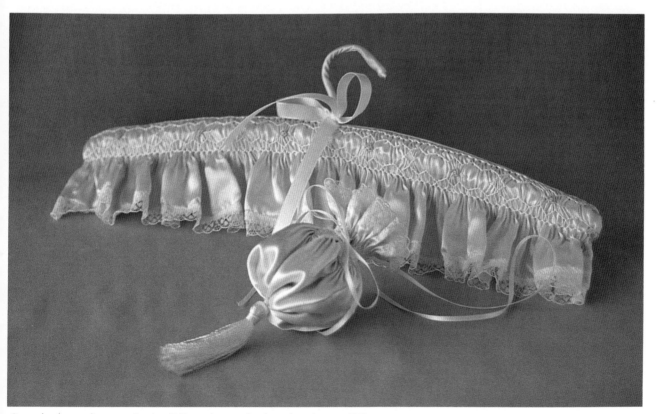

Smocked coathanger (page 54) and smocked sachet (page 58)

Embroidered lingerie case (page 56); below, details of the embroidery

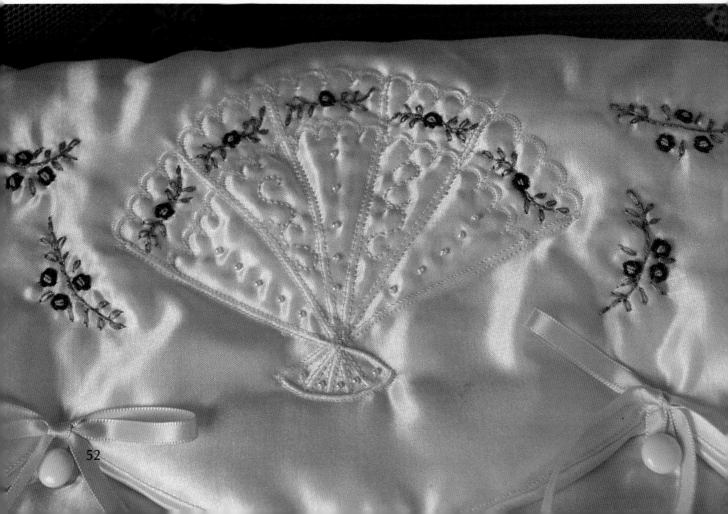

Key for centre panel of guest book cover (page 48)

▨	gold ribbon floss	
ᴠᴠᴠ	light rose	223
▲▲▲	dark rose	315
⁘⁙	pale apricot	819
■	dark green	936
◦◦◦	light green	3052
⊠⊠⊠	bright pink	3354
◣◣◣	pale pink	3713
▨	white	

5
The Honeymoon

Traditionally the first month of marriage, the honeymoon was not always a holiday for the bride and groom unless they were particularly wealthy. As travel became a little easier in Victorian times, the idea of spending a few days away from home became popular, and ranged from a modest stay at the seaside to a full-scale Grand Tour of foreign places.

Smocked Coathanger

Illustrated on page 51

Materials
38 cm long wooden coathanger
17 × 38 cm wadding
20 × 115 cm white satin
1.2 m × 15 mm white flat lace edging
60 cm × 10 mm white satin ribbon
DMC Stranded Cotton, 1 hank each of:
    white
    green 369
    dark apricot 754
    pale apricot 948

1. Fold the strip of wadding in half lengthways and wrap it over the coathanger with the fold at the bottom. Sew the raw edges together, enclosing the coathanger completely.

2. Cut a strip of satin 3 × 12 cm and fold in half lengthways, right sides together. Seam the long edges and turn

through. Slip the tube over the hook of the hanger and secure the bottom end to the wadding. Trim the top 5 mm past the end of the hook, fold the excess back, and glue it to the underside of the hook.

3. Cut a strip of satin 10 × 115 cm and finish the long edges with a narrow or overlocked hem. Pleat 6 rows for smocking, with the first one 2 cm below the top edge. Sew lace edging over the finished edge at the bottom of the strip.

4. Smock the strip of satin following the instructions on the chart, then withdraw all the pleating threads.

5. Cut a strip of satin 9 × 43 cm and pin the smocked panel to it with right sides facing, matching the centres and ends of the fabric, and distributing the gathers evenly. Seam along the line of the top holding thread, leaving a gap of 5 mm at the centre point.

6. Turn the piece to the right side and slip the hook of the hanger through the gap in the stitching. Fold the plain satin strip over the back of the hanger and tuck in the seam allowances at the ends. Narrow-hem the edges of the frill on the smocked section. Slip-stitch the cover in place across the end of the hanger, along the bottom, leaving a 5 cm frill, and up the second side.

7. Tie the satin ribbon in a bow around the base of the hook and trim the ends into an inverted V shape.

Smocking chart for smocked coathanger

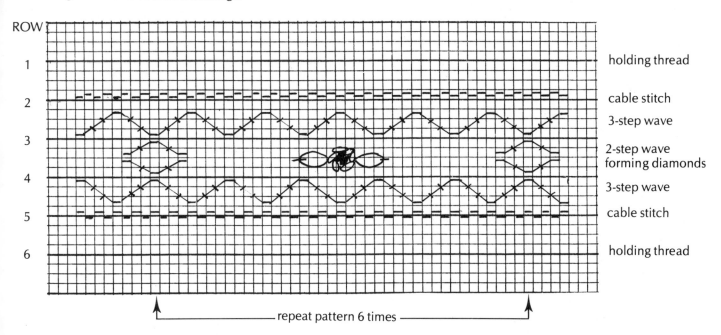

ROW

1 — holding thread

2 — cable stitch

— 3-step wave

3 — 2-step wave forming diamonds

4 — 3-step wave

5 — cable stitch

6 — holding thread

repeat pattern 6 times

Embroider centre of motif with grub roses:

	green	369	lazy daisy stitch
	pale apricot	948	bullion stitch (centre)
	dark apricot	754	bullion stitch (outer petals)

55

Embroidered Lingerie Case

Illustrated on page 52

Materials

40 × 75 cm satin
40 × 75 cm lining fabric
33 × 75 cm wadding
2 × 10 mm buttons
60 cm × 5 mm ribbon
20 × 1 mm seed pearls
DMC Stranded Cotton, 1 hank each of:
   dark rose 315
   green 523
   pale apricot 819
   pink 3716
matching sewing cotton

1. Fold a piece of tracing paper in half and trace the pattern for the flap of the lingerie case from the pattern on page 57. Place the tracing on top of a sheet of white paper and trace the mirror image of the design on the other side of the fold in the paper before opening it out flat. Cut a piece of satin 33 × 75 cm and position it over the traced pattern so that the scalloped line is 2.5 cm from one short edge. Using a fade-out pen, trace the design onto the fabric. Place the satin right side up over the wadding and tack around all the edges. Sew along the lines around the fan using straight stitch on the sewing machine. If your machine can use one, a twin needle gives an especially attractive finish. End all the threads by pulling them through to the back of the work and tying off securely before cutting the excess cotton.
2. Following the stitch diagram, hand embroider the flowers and leaves using the colours as shown. Stitch the two scroll patterns in pale apricot thread using back stitch. Use two strands of cotton for all the embroidery.
3. Sew a pearl bead over each of the dots marked on the design.
4. Cut a lining panel the same size as the satin piece and place it face down over the embroidery. Pin and tack around all the edges, then machine-stitch the layers together. Start at the short end opposite the embroidery and leave a gap of about 12 cm. Turn the panel through to the right side, first clipping the curves and the points between the scallops so that they will lie flat, and slip-stitch the edges of the opening together.
5. Following the diagram, measure a point on either side 24 cm from the plain end of the case and mark the points B with pins. With the wrong sides together, match the points marked A to those marked C, folding the case along the line between the pins. Slip-stitch the two sides together, forming an envelope, and remove the pins. Turn the top embroidered flap down over the lower half of the case.
6. Cut the ribbon into two 30 cm lengths. Fold each one in half and form a loop about 2 cm long by sewing the ribbon together with several small back stitches, leaving 13 cm ends. Stitch the loops firmly to the case at each side of the centre curve, and tie the ends into bows, trimming off any excess ribbon neatly. Sew buttons to the bottom section of the case to correspond with the ribbon loops.

Folding and seaming the lingerie case

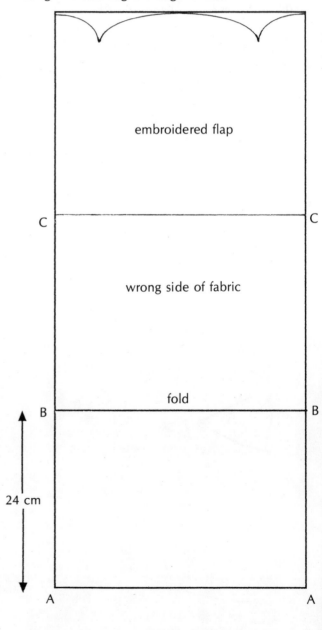

56

Stitch placement diagram for embroidered lingerie case

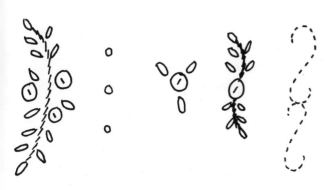

Key

~~	green	523	stem stitch
✴	green	523	lazy daisy stitch
○	pearl bead		
⊖	pink	3716	bullion stitch (centre)
	dark rose	15	bullion stitch (outer petals)
⋮	pale apricot	819	back stitch

Actual size trace pattern for flap of embroidered lingerie case (one half of pattern)

57

Smocked Sachet

Illustrated on page 51

Materials

14 × 65 cm white satin
70 cm white lace edging
1 m × 3 mm white satin ribbon
70 mm white tassel
DMC Stranded Cotton, 1 hank each of:
   white
   green 369
   dark apricot 754
   pale apricot 948
potpourri

1. Finish the long edges of the satin strip with a narrow or overlocked hem. Sew the lace onto one edge, covering the hemstitches.

2. Pleat 5 rows for smocking, starting 2 cm below the lace edge and, following the chart, smock the design.
3. Withdraw the pleating threads and fold the piece in half with right sides together. Seam the short sides, matching the smocked pattern at the stitching line.
4. Gather the long bottom edge of the strip and draw up the gathers tightly. Turn the sachet through to the right side and thread the loop of the tassel through the gathers. Secure it to the inside of the sachet.
5. Thread a length of narrow ribbon through the lower row of chevron stitches shown on the chart. Fill the sachet with a scoop of potpourri and tie the ribbon in a bow, drawing up the top of the sachet to enclose it completely.
6. Use the remaining ribbon to make a hanging loop; fold it in half and sew to the top of the sachet.

Smocking chart for smocked sachet

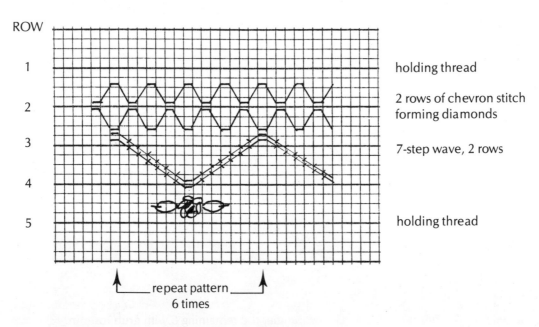

ROW

1 — holding thread

2 — 2 rows of chevron stitch forming diamonds

3 — 7-step wave, 2 rows

4

5 — holding thread

repeat pattern
6 times

Embroider grub roses at the bottom of each wave.

	green	369	lazy daisy stitch
	pale apricot	948	bullion stitch (centres)
	dark apricot	754	bullion stitch (outer petals)

6
Memories

A wedding is long remembered by all concerned and, as an occasion which generates a great deal of emotion, it is natural for even the least sentimental to keep some reminders of the event. Traditionally the bride and groom give gifts to their attendants. Jewellery specially selected for each bridesmaid will be treasured mementoes, and bonbonnières given to guests may form part of a collection which will grow with each wedding and christening attended. The bride may keep her favours, cards and ornaments from the wedding cake. A bouquet of fresh flowers can be preserved, dried or pressed, to make a beautiful picture for the couple's home, and of course the wedding dress and veil can be kept for posterity. The wedding photographs will be shown long after the event; special favourites can be enlarged and framed for either the bride and groom or their parents. A video of the wedding is really the best way to recapture those precious moments, as well as the perfect means of sharing the occasion with friends and relations who were unable to attend. The anniverseraries of the wedding, each with a different traditional gift, will also be a time to remember, and what better way to ensure that the event is not forgotten than with the gift of an embroidered sampler.

Photo Frame with Smocked Bands

Illustrated on page 61

Materials
50 × 25 cm white card
50 cm white satin 115 cm wide
2 m white gathered lace edging, 17 mm wide
24 × 20 cm wadding
60 cm pearl string beading
DMC Stranded Cotton, 1 hank each of:
   dark apricot 754
   pale apricot 948
   green 369
   white

1. Cut a strip of satin 8 cm deep across the width of the fabric. Finish the raw edges with an overlock or zigzag stitch. Pleat 7 rows and smock the design following the chart, completing 14 diamonds in all. Embroider grub roses in the first 6 diamonds, following the colour details given on the chart. Miss the next 2 diamonds, then embroider the remaining 6 with grub roses in the same way. Remove the smocking threads.

2. Cut two 45 cm lengths of lace and pin one along the length of the smocking next to one of the cable rows. Stitch the lace in place, stretching the smocking gently to fit. Repeat on the other side of the smocked band with the second strip of lace. Cut the smocking in half between the two blank diamonds. Turn the edges of the smocked strips to the wrong side and tack them in place using a contrasting thread.

3. Trace the photo frame pattern onto a sheet of white paper. Carefully cut out the centre circle, and use the pattern as a template to cut a piece of white card for the front panel of the frame. Cover the front of the white card with wadding, and carefully cut out a circle from the wadding to match the circle in the card. Retain the paper pattern, which will later be used to line the completed frame.

4. Cover the front panel with a piece of satin fabric, glueing the turnings to the back of the card. Cut the centre circle away leaving 2 cm turnings, then clip these at intervals and glue them down evenly and as smoothly as possible around the centre opening. Trim the edge of the circle with a strip of lace, either sewing or glueing it in place.

5. Following the placement lines marked on the pattern, pin the completed smocked bands in position on the satin-covered front panel. Stitch in place through all fabric layers, and turn the ends of the bands over to the back of the panel. Stitch them in place to the turnings and trim off any excess fabric. Finish the edge of the front panel with a strip of lace sewn all round the edge. Glue the piece of paper used for the pattern to the back of the card, covering all the raw edges, and set the panel aside while preparing the rest of the frame.

6. From the white card cut two rectangles 24.5 × 19.5 cm and cover them with white satin. Use the actual size trace pattern for the stand to cut two pieces of card, and cover these with satin also, taking turnings of 2 cm on each of the 3 longer sides and leaving an allowance of 5 cm on the short top edge, which is not glued down over the cardboard. Pierce a hole through one piece of card at the point marked on the pattern and thread the narrow ribbon through it, knotting the end on the wrong side so that it will not pull through. Glue the two stand sections together, including the extra fabric at the top.

7. Align the centre of the base of the stand with the centre of one short side of one of the covered rectangles and pierce a hole through the card to correspond with the one in the stand. Thread the other end of the narrow ribbon through this, and knot the end at the back. Using the stand section as a guide, mark a line on the back of the frame to correspond with the top edge of the cardboard on the stand. Cut a slit in the rectangular panel of card the exact width of the top edge of the stand, and push the fabric overlap through it. Glue the overlap down flat on the back of the card, then glue the two satin-covered cards together with their wrong sides facing.

8. Take the completed front section of the frame and glue it to the front of the back section on three sides only; the fourth side is left open to allow for the insertion and removal of the photograph.

Smocking chart for photo frame with smocked bands

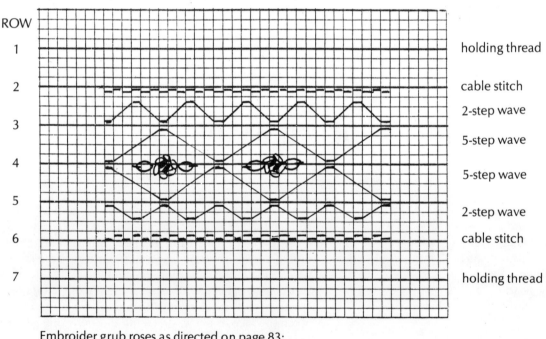

ROW	
1	holding thread
2	cable stitch
	2-step wave
3	5-step wave
4	5-step wave
5	2-step wave
6	cable stitch
7	holding thread

Embroider grub roses as directed on page 83:

⬭	green	369	lazy daisy stitch
⸰	dark apricot	754	bullion stitch (centre)
⸰⸰	pale apricot	948	bullion stitch (outer petals)

60

Photo frame with smocked bands
(page 59)

Ribbon-weave photo album
(page 66)

Above: Ribbon-weave heart box (page 68); below, smocked keepsake box (page 71)

Cross-stitch wedding sampler (page 72)

Video slipcase (page 76) and découpage greetings card (page 44)

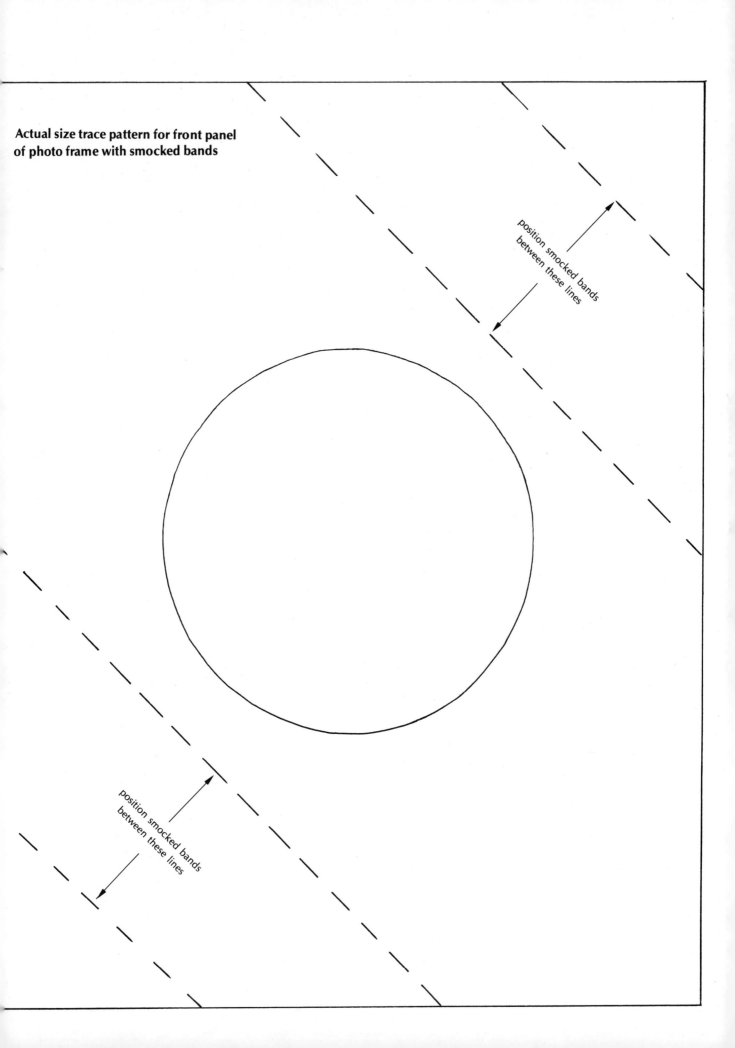

Actual size trace pattern for front panel of photo frame with smocked bands

position smocked bands between these lines

position smocked bands between these lines

Actual size trace pattern for photograph frame stand

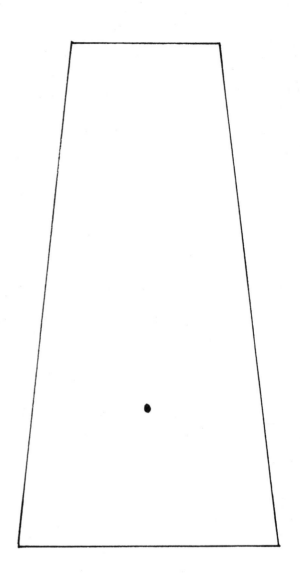

Ribbon-weave Photo Album

Illustrated on page 61

Materials
20 cm square iron-on interfacing
4.5 m × 7 mm white ribbon
4.5 m × 10 mm white ribbon
50 cm white satin cord
artificial flowers and leaves
white florist's tape
photo album 25.5 × 28.5 cm
50 cm square wadding
2 pieces thin card 22.5 × 28.5 cm
50 cm white satin 115 cm wide
1.8 m × 22 mm gathered lace edging
spray glue
craft glue

1. Spray the outside of the album lightly with glue and cover it with a piece of wadding 50 × 30 cm. Trim the edges of the wadding level with the outer edges of the cover and set aside to dry.
2. Cut a piece of satin 60 × 40 cm and place the album, opened, on the wrong side of the fabric. Clip the fabric either side of the spine and trim off a small piece between the cuts, leaving about 1.5 cm to turn over into the spine. Glue the satin in place all round the edges of the cover, taking care to leave enough 'give' to allow the album to close properly.
3. Glue gathered lace edging all around the edge of the cover on the wrong side.
4. Cover the two rectangles of thin card with satin,

glueing the turnings neatly in place, then glue these covered cards in place inside the front and back covers of the album, covering the raw edges of the satin and the bound edge of the lace. Set the album aside while preparing the decorative front panel.

5. Prepare a square of ribbon-weaving as directed in Chapter 7, cutting 20 cm strips of ribbon and alternating the widths as they are pinned across the interfacing.

6. Trace the heart shape from the diagram and use it to cut a piece from the remaining wadding. Transfer the heart pattern to the back of the ribbon-weave panel, with the point of the heart towards one corner so that the ribbons run diagonally across the shape. Machine stitch around the line of the heart, then cut out the shape 0.5 cm outside the stitching.

7. Stitch the remaining gathered lace around the edge of the heart-shaped panel, then lightly glue the piece of wadding to the back. Turn the raw edges of the ribbon-weaving to the back and pin it in place on the front of the covered album.

8. Slip-stitch the ribbon-weave heart shape to the album cover as neatly as possible, then glue the satin cord around the edge of the heart, starting and finishing at the centre top of the shape.

9. Make up a small spray of flowers and leaves, binding them together with florist's tape. Trim the stem ends to about 2.5 cm and add a bow of 17 mm wide ribbon. Glue the completed spray firmly to the top of the heart.

Actual size trace pattern for ribbon-weave heart panel for photo album

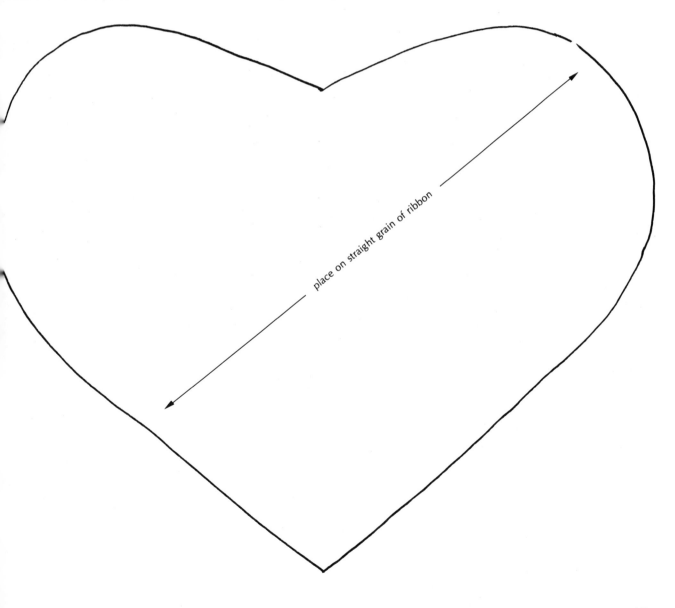

place on straight grain of ribbon

Ribbon-weave Heart Box

Illustrated on page 62

Materials

30 × 50 cm white card for box
30 × 50 cm thin white card
30 cm satin fabric 115 cm wide
30 cm white lining taffeta 115 cm wide
50 cm pearl string beading
artificial flowers and leaves
white florist's tape
craft glue
20 cm square wadding
20 cm square iron-on interfacing
white ribbons for woven panel—6 m of 7 mm wide;
   3 m of 10 mm wide; 1.5 m of 24 mm wide

1. Prepare the ribbon-weave panel for the top of the box following the general instructions in Chapter 7. Cut the ribbons into 20 cm lengths; start pinning across the top of the interfacing with a 7 mm wide ribbon, followed by ribbons in the sequence 24 mm, 7 mm, 10 mm, 7 mm, three times. Pin the remaining ribbons down the left hand side in the same sequence. Complete the weaving as directed and set aside while making the box.

2. From the white card cut the following pieces:
   heart for box lid from pattern A
   heart for box base from pattern B
   side lid strip 3 × 46 cm (score a line at the centre and fold in half)
   box side strip 9 × 44.5 cm (score and bend as for the box lid)
From thin white card cut the following lining sections:
   heart for lid lining from pattern C
   heart for base lining from pattern D
   side lining strip 6.5 × 43 cm (score and bend this strip in the centre)

3. Lightly glue wadding to hearts A, C and D.

4. Draw round the edge of heart A onto the back of the ribbon-weaving and machine a line of straight stitch on this line. Cut out the shape 1.5 cm outside the machined line; centre the cardboard heart on the reverse of the ribbon-weaving, with the wadding side down. Glue the turnings to the back of the card, clipping the edge of the fabric where necessary to allow it to lie flat. Glue down any loose ends of ribbon and set the piece aside to dry.

5. Cover the base piece of the box smoothly with a piece of satin, clipping curves and easing to fit where necessary. Cover the side strip in the same way. Ladder stitch the short ends of the strip together, then fold it on the scored lines to form the point of the heart shape. Pin the base in position onto the side strip with the seam at the centre top of the heart, curving the card gently into shape. Stitch securely all round the edge with a doubled length of sewing cotton.

6. Line the box by cutting a piece of taffeta 48 × 12 cm. Press a 2 cm turning to the wrong side on one long edge. Glue this turning to the back of the card strip, then glue down one short edge. Roll the strip up lightly and run a line of glue around the inside of the box, 0.5 cm down from the top. Starting at the top of the heart, glue the raw edge of the lining strip in place and gently unroll the strip, pressing it firmly into the glue all round the edges. Glue the neatened edge down to cover the first lining edge, tucking in any folds at the corners as neatly as possible. Lightly glue the bottom turnings around the base of the box.

7. Cover the base lining heart with taffeta. This can then be glued in place if desired by first coating the inside box base with adhesive and then pushing the covered shape gently into position.

8. To make the box lid cut a piece of satin 9 × 50 cm, fold it in half lengthways and press. Slip the cardboard strip inside the fabric and, keeping the edge to the fold, turn in the seam allowances at each end, glueing them in place on the inside of the shape. Join the short ends with ladder stitch then attach the lid top in the same way as making up the box in step 5. Glue the seam allowances flat to the underside of the lid, clipping where necessary to reduce the bulk. Cover the lid lining heart with taffeta, and glue it in position to cover all raw edges.

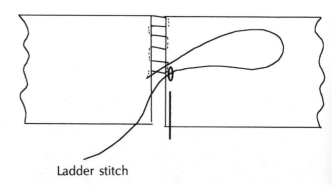

Ladder stitch

9. Decorate the lid of the box with a length of pearl string glued securely around the edge, starting and finishing at the centre top of the heart shape. Make up a spray of flowers and leaves, binding the stems together with florist's tape. Trim the stems to about 2.5 cm, then tie a length of 24 mm wide ribbon in a bow just below the flowers. Glue the completed spray to the top of the box lid.

Actual size trace patterns for ribbon-weave heart box

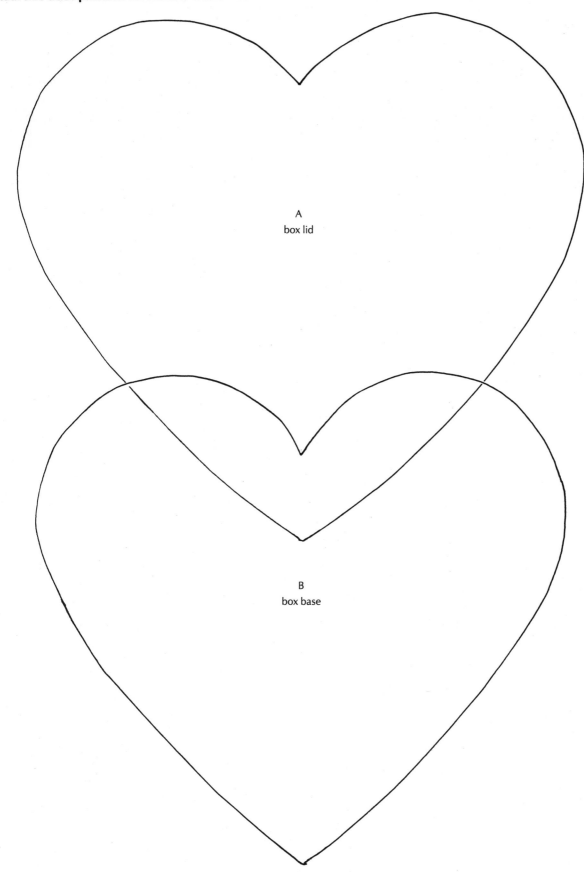

A
box lid

B
box base

Actual size trace patterns for ribbon-weave heart box linings

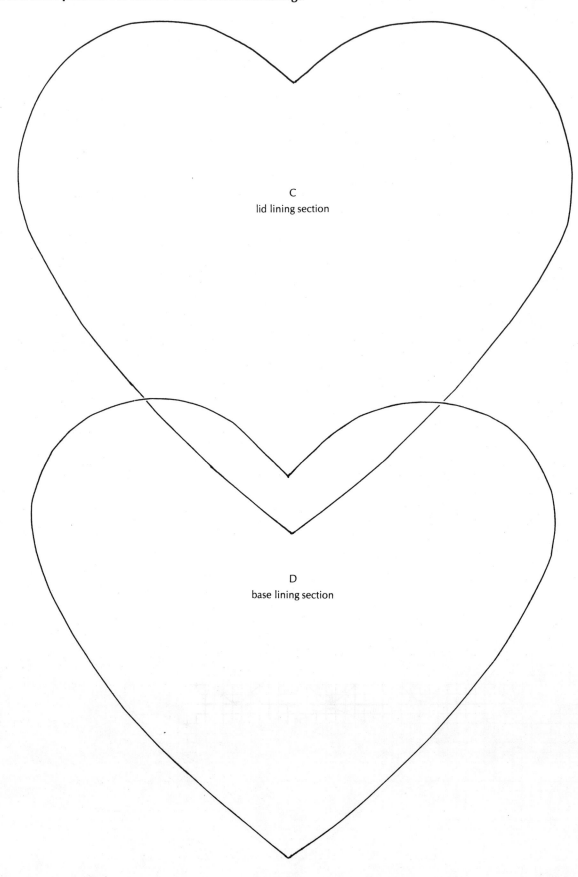

C
lid lining section

D
base lining section

Smocked Keepsake Box

Illustrated on page 62

Materials

1 large sheet white card
75 × 12 cm thin white card
30 × 50 cm wadding
80 × 115 cm white satin
50 × 115 cm white taffeta lining fabric
3 m × 17 mm white lace edging
54 white pearl beads, 3 mm diameter
white sewing cotton
craft glue
25 cm × 15 mm pearl fringe
DMC Stranded Cotton, 1 hank of white

1. Cut 2 strips of satin 12 × 115 cm and join them together along one short side, with right sides facing. Finish the raw edges with an overlocked or narrow hem and pleat 9 rows for smocking using 1.5 m long threads. Spread the pleats on one long edge and sew on the lace to cover the hem stitching. Pull up the gathers again ready for smocking and tie off and trim the ends of the thread.
2. Following the chart, smock the satin strip, starting with row 2 nearest to the plain edge. Repeat the heart pattern 18 times in all. When complete, remove all the gathering threads except the holding thread on row 1.
3. Cut the following pieces from white card:
    1 circle 24 cm diameter
    2 circles 23.5 cm diameter
    1 circle 7.5 cm diameter
    75 × 12.5 cm strip for box side
    78 × 3 cm strip for box lid
4. Cover all the circles except one of the 23.5 cm diameter ones with wadding. Cut two circles of lining fabric 30 cm in diameter and use these to cover the wadding on the 24 cm circle and the 23.5 cm circle. Glue the edges in place on the wrong side of each section. Cover the remaining circles with satin in the same way. Cover the box side strip with satin.
5. Assemble the base of the box by ladder-stitching the short sides of the satin-covered card together. Pin the satin-covered 23.5 cm card without wadding over one end of the tube thus formed and sew it firmly into position. Line the box with a strip of taffeta 80 × 19 cm

Smocking chart for smocked keepsake box

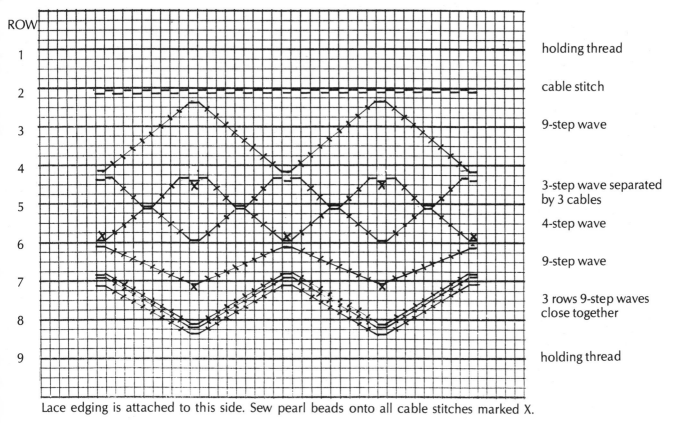

ROW	
1	holding thread
2	cable stitch
3	9-step wave
4	3-step wave separated by 3 cables
5	4-step wave
6	9-step wave
7	3 rows 9-step waves close together
8	
9	holding thread

Lace edging is attached to this side. Sew pearl beads onto all cable stitches marked X.

mounted on the 75 × 12 cm piece of thin card. Glue the turnings down on one long edge and one short one only. Glue the long edge in place 1 cm below the top edge of the box, starting with the unfinished short end, and complete the lining by glueing the finished short edge down to cover the raw edges. Glue the bottom turnings lightly to the base of the box. Press the lining-covered 23.5 cm circle of card into the box to complete the base lining.

6. To make the lid, cut a strip of satin 82 × 12 cm and fold it in half lengthways. Insert the narrow card strip and adjust the satin so that the seam allowances at each end are folded to one side of the strip; this will be inside the box when complete. Pin the seam allowances on the long edges together right next to the cardboard, and sew along that line with small running stitches to hold the card in place. Seam the two short ends together. Push the 24 cm circle of card into the ring formed by the strip so that the finished side of the card faces downwards and the seam allowances of both pieces rest on the top. Stitch the seam allowances together through all thicknesses with a herringbone stitch, easing the line of running stitches around the edge strip just up over the top of the lid.

7. Seam the short ends of the smocked strip together, matching the pattern, and trim off excess fabric. Sew on the last bead to complete the pattern. Draw up the holding thread tightly and flatten the piece to form a circle. Knot the ends securely and cut off excess. Pin the smocking to the lid of the box, making sure the pattern is spread evenly, and leaving the lace edging to overhang the outer edge. Slip-stitch the smocking in place through the hem underneath the lace and the satin at the edge of the box lid side piece. Glue the pleated edges at the centre of the smocking securely to the cardboard.

8. Glue the small satin-covered circle of card to the centre of the box lid, covering the raw edges of the smocked strip completely. Glue a line of pearl fringe trim around the edge of this circle.

Cross-stitch Wedding Sampler

Illustrated on page 63

Materials
35 × 60 cm white Aida fabric, 11 holes per inch
DMC Stranded Cotton, 1 hank each of:
  light rose 223
  dark rose 315
  pale green 524
  very dark blue 791
  dark blue 792
  French blue 793
  medium blue 794
  bright blue 799
  light blue 800
  pale peach 819
  dark green 936
  bright pink 962
  mid green 3052
  light pink 3713
  sugar pink 3716

1. Prepare the fabric by overlocking the raw edges to prevent them from fraying and marking the centre lines of the design with a row of tacking stitches in each direction.

2. Following the chart work the design in three strands of thread throughout.

3. Using the lettering chart and spare graph lines provided on page 76, work out the desired lettering; fill in the letters leaving one space between each. Count the number of squares occupied by the entire name and divide in half to find the centre; mark this point with arrows. Occasionally a chart will not fit evenly either side of the centre line of the chart; in this case an extra space must be added to the shorter side. Put next to a straight letter, e.g. t, l or h, this will not be noticeable. Try to avoid putting the extra space after open letters such as c or r or large ones such as m or w, where it may look out of place.

4. Matching the centre arrows to the centre line of the fabric, embroider the desired names in the places indicated on the chart, followed by the date along the bottom line.

5. Lightly press the completed embroidery on the wrong side with a damp cloth, then mount and frame as desired.

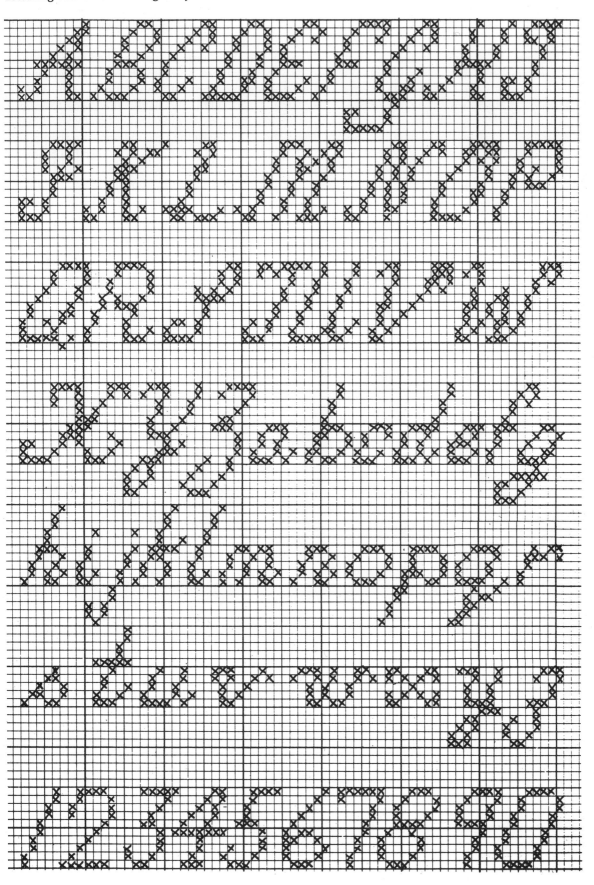

Working chart for wedding sampler
(each square on the graph represents one stitch)

Key

light rose	223				
dark rose	315				
pale green	524				
very dark blue	791				
dark blue	792				
French blue	793				
medium blue	794				
bright blue	799				
light blue	800				
pale peach	819				
dark green	936				
bright pink	962				
mid green	3052				
light pink	3713				
sugar pink	3716				

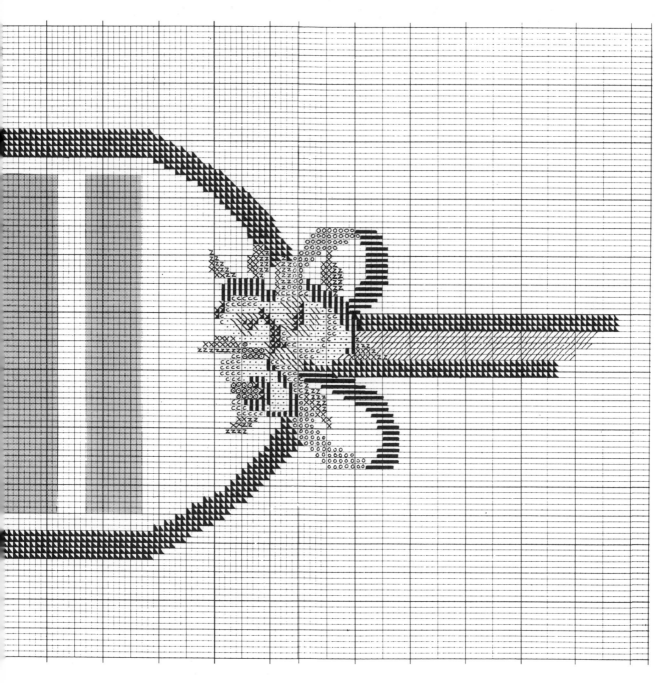

Spare graph lines for charting lettering

centre

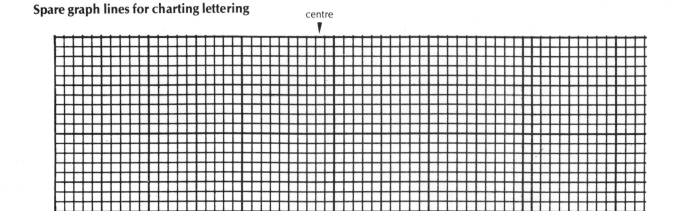

centre

Video Slipcase

Illustrated on page 64

Materials
35 × 27 cm plastic canvas, 10 holes per 2.5 cm
Craftlon craft ribbon, 1 reel each of
   white 1
   burgundy 10
1 reel gold ribbon floss

1. Use the lettering chart on page 78 to work out the charts for the desired names and pencil them in on the shaded area of the chart for the front of the video case.
2. Count four threads from the top and side edges at one corner of the sheet of plastic canvas to establish the starting point for the embroidery. Following the chart, on which each square represents one stitch, work the design for the front of the video case in tent stitch, using the threads and colours as shown. Ribbon floss should be used double to cover the canvas properly.
3. Refer to the layout diagram on page 79, on which each square represents two meshes of the canvas, and work the back panel of the cover in cushion stitch over 4

threads, 10 × 18 blocks, using white Craftlon ribbon. Outline this with a row of tent stitch in the same yarn, then a second row of tent stitch in gold ribbon floss.
4. Work the spine of the case as shown on the chart, using burgundy Craftlon ribbon in satin stitch for the heart motifs and white for the remaining stitchery. Stitch the border rows in tent stitch, using white and gold for alternate rows.
5. Stitch the two sections for the top and bottom panels in mosaic stitch over 2 threads of canvas, using alternate rows of gold and white, 21 × 4 blocks. Outline each section with a row of gold tent stitch.
6. When all the stitchery is complete, cut out each section of the case with a border of one unworked thread of canvas showing all round. Place the top panel to the back of the front section with wrong sides facing, and line up the holes along the edges. Stitch the pieces together with white Craftlon ribbon using an overcasting stitch through each pair of holes. Attach the bottom section to the front panel in the same way, then sew the

Working chart for video slipcase front panel
(each square on the graph represents one stitch)

Key

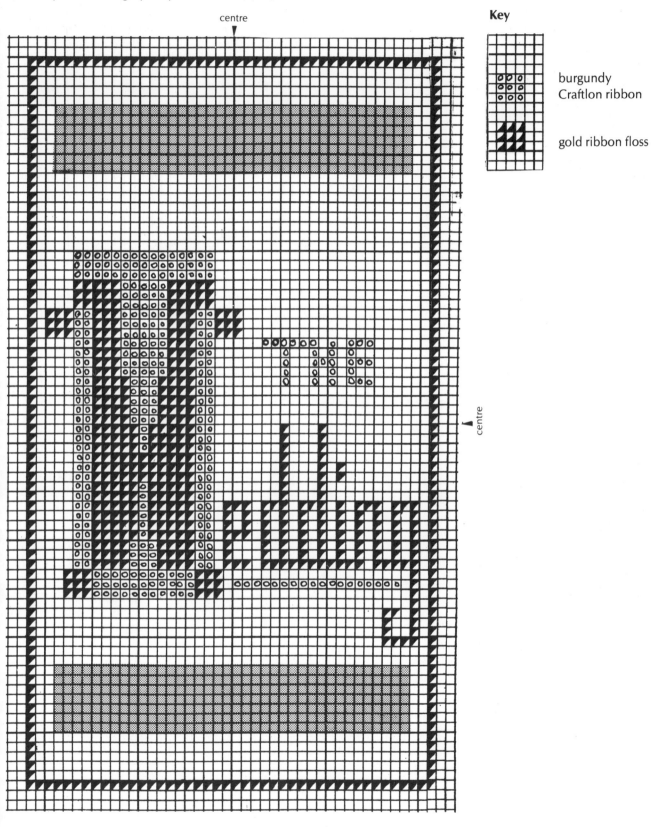

burgundy
Craftlon ribbon

gold ribbon floss

spine section in place on the left-hand side of the cover, joining it at top and bottom to the end panels.

7. Attach the back section of the slipcase to the side and spine sections in the same way, working around the three sides. Complete the case by oversewing the unworked canvas around the opening with white Craftlon ribbon.

Note The slipcase is designed to be a little oversize so that the normal plastic cover which protects the video will fit into it as well. If you desire a tighter fit, omit the outer borders of gold tent stitch when embroidering the 5 sections, and use gold ribbon floss to join the sections together instead of the white Craftlon ribbon.

Lettering chart for video slipcase

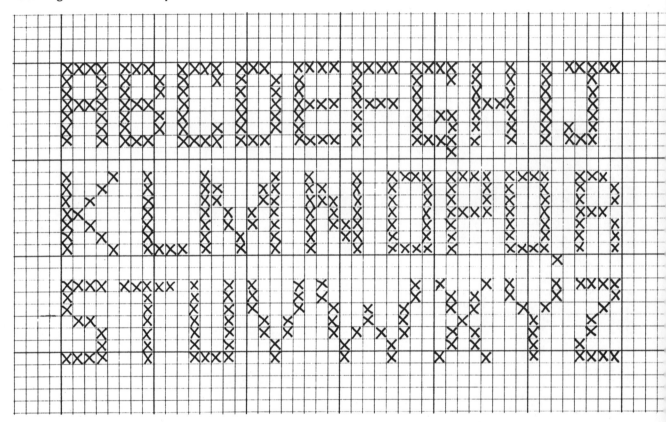

Spare graph lines for charting lettering

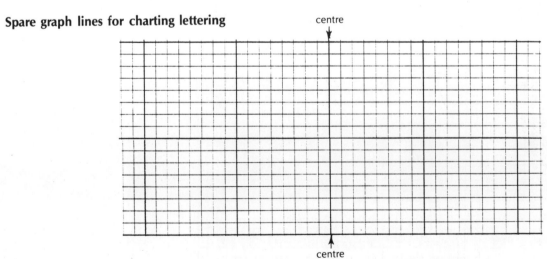

Working chart for video slipcase spine

Key

burgundy Craftlon ribbon	satin stitch
white Craftlon ribbon	slanted satin stitch
white Craftlon ribbon	tent stitch
gold ribbon floss	tent stitch

Layout diagram for video slipcase
(each square on the chart represents 2 threads of the plastic canvas)

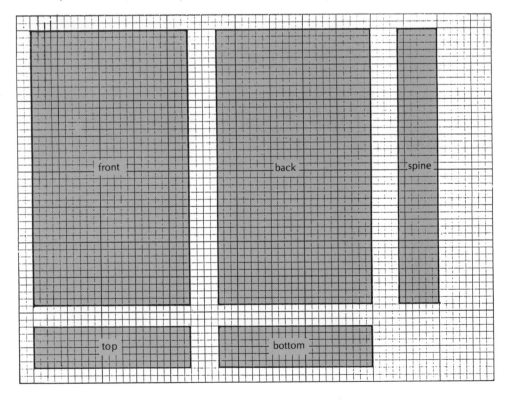

7
Techniques

Ribbon Weaving

The dimensions of interfacing and quantities of ribbon required are given in the instructions for individual projects. Once a panel of ribbon weaving has been completed, it can be used like a piece of ordinary fabric, even to the extent of being incorporated into clothing. Often a prepared panel will be sufficient for more than one project, and even comparatively small scraps can be made into attractive potpourri sachets or pincushions. Braids and lace can be used as well as many different types of ribbon, the main requirement being that they are able to stand the heat required to fuse them to the interfacing. It is a good idea to use ordinary dressmaking pins rather than those with coloured heads, which can melt should they come in contact with a hot iron; a pressing sheet designed for use in preparing appliqué will also help to prevent the iron coming in contact with the glue on the interfacing.

To prepare a panel of ribbon weaving, cut a piece of interfacing according to the dimensions given in the pattern for the project and place it glue side up on an ironing board. Cut the ribbons to the lengths specified in the project instructions and, starting 2 cm in from the left-hand edge, pin them side by side across the top of the interfacing, alternating their widths as indicated in the pattern.

When the right-hand edge of the interfacing is reached, start to pin the remaining ribbons down the left-hand side of the piece, 2 cm down from the top. When all the ribbons are in place, weave each crosswise ribbon in turn under and over the lengthwise ones, going under the first one on each alternate row, and pinning down each end on the right-hand side as the weaving is completed. Gently ease the ribbons into place so that they lie flat and straight, then heat the iron and fuse them to the interfacing. Once the glue has started to take effect the pins can be removed and the piece turned over to allow a firmer pressing on the back to finish off.

After the ribbon weaving has cooled, the shapes to be cut out should be drawn on the back of the interfacing in pencil and then machine-stitched around the edges to ensure that the ribbons cannot move out of place.

Needlepoint and Cross-stitch

Both these types of counted thread embroidery are worked from charts. For cross-stitch and the basic tent stitch designs in needlepoint, each square on a chart represents one stitch, and the different symbols indicate the thread colours which are used. Needlepoint charts, such as those for the border of the guest book and the needlepoint shoe clips, use the lines of the graph to represent the grid of the canvas, with the lines showing the stitches used in the positions in which they should be embroidered.

Counted thread embroidery techniques use a blunt needle to avoid piercing the background threads while stitching. These are available in several sizes, with the thickness of thread to be used and the size of the holes in the canvas being the main consideration when choosing the most appropriate one to use.

Basic Needlepoint Stitches

Back stitch
Worked in a line in any direction over one or two threads, back stitch is used for finer details and outlining. Charts show the exact length and angle of the stitches used.

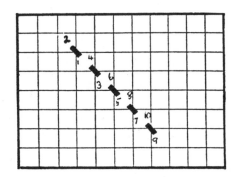

Basketweave tent stich
Work in diagonal rows from top right to bottom left over all intersections of the canvas. The stitch takes its name from the pattern made on the back of the work, and is the basic 'tapestry' stitch used on canvas.

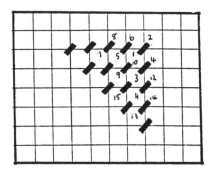

Beaded tent stitch
Each stitch is worked diagonally over one intersection of the canvas, from the bottom left to the top right, leaving a long diagonal thread across the back of the work. One or more beads, as required, are threaded onto the stitch as it is being worked. The stitch is best worked using a fine beading needle and a strong thread which is specially produced for the purpose.

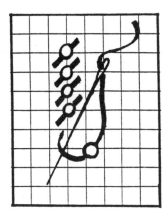

Cross-stitch (see diagram on page 82)
This stitch can be worked in rows by embroidering the first stitches in a line from left to right, then working back in the opposite direction to complete the row, or as single stitches. For large areas it is better to work in rows, as the finished effect tends to be smoother.

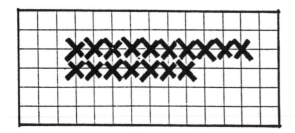

Cushion stitch

A simple but effective stitch which is made up of satin-stitched blocks consisting of diagonal stitches over 1,2,3,4,3,2 and 1 threads. Alternate blocks are worked in opposite directions, and the pattern is very striking when worked on contrasting colours.

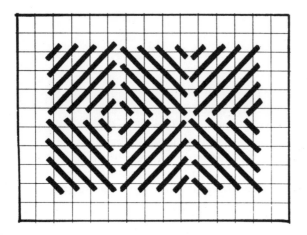

Mosaic stitch

A simple stitch composed of groups of three diagonal stitches worked over 1,2 and 1 threads of canvas, forming a small square block pattern. It looks very attractive when worked in two colours.

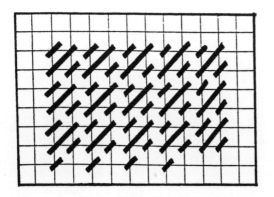

Satin stitch (straight stitch)

Charts for the individual projects will indicate over how many threads these blocks of straight stitches must be worked. Blocks of stitches can be made vertically, horizontally or diagonally, depending on the effect required. The length of the stitches is also subject to variation; the charts for the projects specify over how many threads a stitch should be worked.

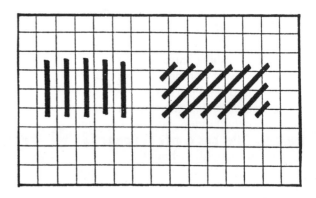

Tent stitch

The basic 'tapestry' stitch, tent stitch should not be confused with half cross-stitch, which looks the same on the front of the work but has a straight stitch on the back of the canvas. Tent stitch has a long diagonal stitch on the back and uses more thread than half cross, but is much more durable. Lines of tent stitch can be worked in any direction, but for filling large areas of canvas it is best to use the basket-weave variation.

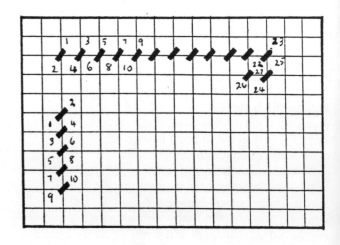

Embroidery Stitches

The patterns in this book use some very simple basic embroidery stitches. Use a fine crewel needle with a sharp point; most patterns only require two or three strands of stranded cotton or gold thread. Cut thread to lengths of about 40 cm, or even less when using metallic threads, as they tend to wear quickly when being worked.

Starting and finishing threads

A very neat way of starting and finishing threads in soft embroidery is to use a pin stitch. This is a tiny back stitch taken over no more than two threads of the fabric, which is subsequently hidden by the first stitches of the embroidery. The thread may be finished off in a similar way, with the pin stitch buried beneath the stitchery. Alternatively, the thread may be finished off by weaving it neatly through the back of several stitches on the wrong side of the fabric.

Back stitch

Work from right to left. Start by bringing the needle up through the fabric a stitch-length in from the end of the line to be embroidered, and put the needle back down into the fabric right at the end of the line. The second stitch is made by bringing the thread through a stitch-length to the left, and inserting the needle into the hole at the start of the previous stitch.

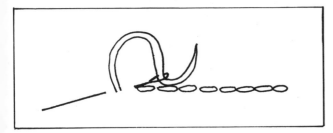

Bullion stitch roses

A single bullion stitch is worked as shown in the diagram. Bring the thread out at point B, then take the needle to point A and insert it through the fabric, coming out again at B. Wrap the thread firmly but not tightly over the point of the needle several times, until the wraps equal the length of the space between A and B. Holding the wrapped thread down firmly with your thumb, pull the needle through the loops and gently stroke the wrapped thread into place.

   The rose is constructed from a number of bullion stitches. Start in the centre with 2 stitches in one of the petal shades lying next to each other, then surround these with a spiral formation of about 5 more stitches in a slightly different shade of thread.

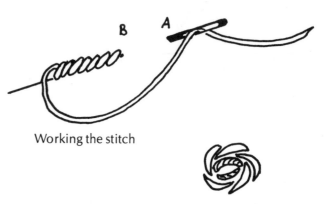

Working the stitch

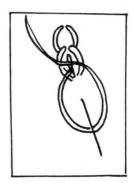

Completed bullion stitch rose

Chain stitch

Start by bringing the needle out at the beginning of the line to be worked. The needle is put back into the same hole and the point is taken out again a short distance below, with the yarn passing underneath it. Pulling the needle through forms a loop. The next stitch is made in the same way, with the needle entering the fabric inside the loop at the point where the yarn is emerging.

French knots (see diagram on page 84)

The needle is brought out at the starting point and the thread is wrapped around the point of the needle one or more times in an anti-clockwise direction. The point of the needle is put into the fabric close to or even into the starting point; the loops are held down firmly with the thumbnail of the left hand while the needle is pulled through to the wrong side.

Lazy daisy stitch (see diagram on page 84)

The thread is brought out at the starting point and the needle is inserted into the same hole, emerging a short distance away with the thread looped underneath it. The loop is pulled to lie flat on the fabric, and anchored with a small straight stitch. The stitches can be worked singly or in groups to represent the petals of larger flowers.

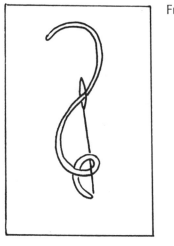
French knot

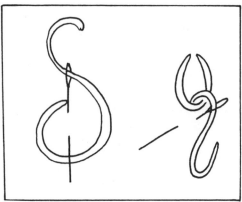
Lazy daisy stitch

Satin stitch

This is a very useful filling stitch in which long straight stitches are worked next to each other to fill the area being worked. Care should be taken to make sure that the stitches are evenly spaced, just touching each other.

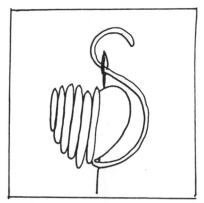

Stem stitch

The needle is inserted into the fabric half a stitch length from the end of the last stitch and brought out next to the previous stitch with the loop of thread kept underneath the needle. A line of stitches is produced, with each one overlapping the one before it.

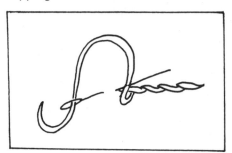

Smocking

The smocking designs in this book are all shown in the form of charts. The pleating threads are represented by heavy horizontal lines, and the pleats themselves are the vertical lines. The stitches are drawn in showing the number of pleats and the distance between the pleating threads occupied by each pattern segment. The explanation at the end of each pattern row tells you the number and type of stitches to be used to build each design.

Pleating is easily done using a smocking machine; if one is not available, then transfer dots should be used. Many needlework shops now offer a pleating service for their clients.

Smocking is generally worked with three strands of stranded cotton in a fine sharp-pointed crewel needle. The patterns in this book use only three basic stitches, which are detailed below. Several patterns are enhanced with grub-rose embroidery, instructions for which can be found on page 83.

Smocking is one of the few embroidery techniques where it is possible to start and finish with a knot in the cotton. To begin stitching, tie a knot in the end of the thread, and pass the needle through the fabric from the back to the front between the third and fourth pleats from the left-hand edge of the work. Take the thread through the third pleat from right to left; the needle is now in the correct position to make the first stitch.

When finishing a thread, make a small stitch through the back of the pleat just worked, looping the thread around the needle so that a knot forms as it is drawn through. A second knot can be made on top of the first for extra security if desired. Clip the end of the thread close to the knot for a neat finish.

Basic Smocking Stitches

Cable stitch

With the needle held at right angles to the pleats and parallel to the pleating thread, take the needle through the next pleat to the right from right to left. Keeping the thread above the needle, pull it through to tighten the stitch across the two pleats.

The second stitch is made by taking the needle through the next pleat from right to left, but with the thread passing below the needle. Continue in this way across the row of pleats, alternating the position of the thread on each stitch. Use the pleating thread as a guide to keep the line of stitches straight.

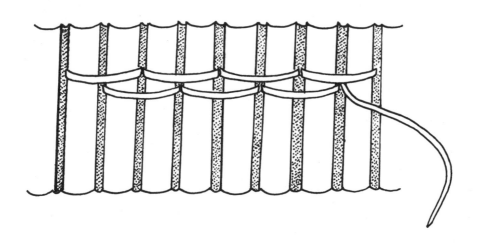

Chevron stitch

This stitch is started with a cable stitch on the line of the pleating thread at the bottom of the pattern. The second stitch is made with the thread held below the needle, picking up the next pleat to the right halfway between two pleating threads. After pulling the thread through, the next stitch is made horizontally through the next pleat, with the thread above the needle. The pattern is completed by taking the next stitch downwards to the starting line. Continue in this way across the entire row. To form a diamond pattern the work is turned upside-down and a second row worked next to the first in the same way.

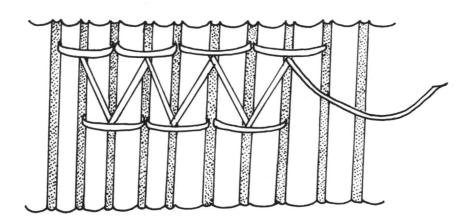

Wave stitch

This stitch starts with a cable stitch on the line of the pleating thread at the bottom of the row. The space between this and the next pleating thread is then divided into the number of steps in the wave required by the individual pattern. The illustration shows a three-step wave, in which three stitches are taken, each with the thread kept below the needle, and each one-third of the distance between the pleating threads. The next stitch is a cable stitch made parallel to the top pleating thread, with the cotton held above the needle. The second section of the wave is made in the same way as the first, with the working thread kept above the needle for the three descending stitches. Repeating these steps across the work forms the pattern. Like chevron stitch, a wave pattern can also be used to form a diamond trellis pattern by working a second, mirror-image row with the work held upside-down.

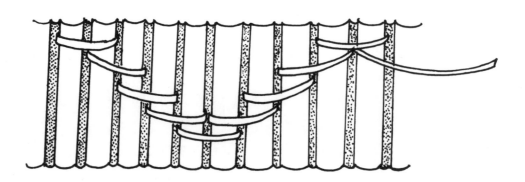

Making Decorative Floral Sprays

Floristry is a craft which needs many hours of practice before it can be mastered. Many aspects of design and colour coordination are part of it, as well as the practical aspects of handling living flowers and foliage. The projects in this book all use silk flowers, although fresh ones could be substituted if required, and the designs have been kept fairly simple. (Bouquets and posies are best left to professional florists as they are very time-consuming and require special wiring techniques which are beyond the scope of this book.) To simplify the construction of these floral decorations, each of the projects is illustrated with a line drawing and a placement diagram. These all adopt the convention of starting with the element at the top of the page, even where this will be at the bottom of the finished piece. Each flower, leaf or spray is taped to the one before it in the order shown, leaving a short length of stem between them. Florist's tape sticks to itself when stretched thinly, and care should be taken to keep the stems as thin as possible while still making sure the flowers are securely joined together. They are then arranged to hide the wires,

without crowding the flowers together so much that they become crushed. The item shown in a box at the top of the placement diagram is the starting point; the final flower is also shown in a box, and the stem line shows below it in most of the arrangements. Details of how to finish the stems are included in the separate instructions for each project.

The bride's head-dress and the bridesmaid's hair comb are both symmetrical arrangements and are made in two identical halves, starting with the elements detailed in the square boxes. The two sections are joined in the middle, and the join is covered with the flower shown in the circular box. Excess stem wire should be trimmed and all exposed ends of wire should be covered with tape.

In projects which do not include details of the arrangements, a simple gathering together of a few flowers and leaves is all that is necessary. Bind the stems together with fine wire or tape, and cover any bare wire with florist's tape in a colour which matches the stems.

Further Reading

Embroidery and Crafts
Needlepoint Techniques and Projects, Jenni Kirkham
Découpage with Scrapbook Pictures, Vivienne Garforth
Stitches for Embroidery, Heather Joynes
How to Bead, Maisie Jarratt
Embroidery Beading Designs and Techniques, Maisie Jarratt
Smocking Ideas, Fiona Roediger

Millinery
Hats for Brides and Weddings, Margo-Ann Daly
Hats on Heads, Mildred Anlezark

Floristry
Flower Arrangements for Weddings, Barbara Coates

All these titles are published by Kangaroo Press.

Suppliers

Gilbert Bridal Floral & Handcraft
306 Murray Street
Perth WA 6000
Mail order service

Craft supplies
Cake decorations
Wedding flowers
Craftlon ribbon
Embroidery threads and fabric
Plastic canvas

Creative Bead Imports
Fremantle Craft & Supplies
Delicate Stitches
225 South Terrace
South Fremantle WA 6162
Mail order service

Beads
Lace appliqués
Smocking supplies
Needlepoint supplies
Embroidery threads

Lingtrim Enterprises Pty Ltd
37 St Edmonds Road
Prahran Vic 3181
Manufacturer
Craftlon ribbon is available nationally in craft and variety stores.

Craftlon ribbon

Lincraft
103–111 Stanley Street
West Melbourne Vic 3003

Branches in most states

Retailer of craft supplies
Fabrics
Bridal lace, trims and beads
Perforated paper

DMC Needlecraft Pty Ltd
PO Box 317
Earlwood NSW 2206
Wholesaler
DMC products are widely available in retail stores and craft shops throughout Australia.

DMC Embroidery threads
Cross-stitch fabrics

Anne's Glory Box
60 Beaumont Street
Hamilton
Newcastle NSW 2303
Mail order service

General sewing and craft supplies

Country Bumpkin
76A Kensington Road
Rose Park
South Australia 5067
Mail order service

Smocking supplies
Pleating service

Madeira (Australia) Pty Ltd
25–27 Izett Street
Prahran Vic 3181
Wholesale distributor

Madeira embroidery threads

Needle Art and Wools
7a Cinema City Arcade
Hay Street
Perth WA 6000
Mail order service

DMC threads
Embroidery fabric and supplies

Rannelle Designs
3 Leaf Close
Middle Park Qld 4074
Mail order service

Greetings card blanks

Swanland Crafts
PO Box 228
Belmont WA 6104
Mail order service

Greetings card blanks

Judith & Kathryn
11 Avenue Road
Highgate SA 5063

Hand-painted angel heads

Index